REVENUE MANAGEMENT

REVENUE MANAGEMENT

Hard-core Tactics for Market Domination

ROBERT G. CROSS

BROADWAY BOOKS
NEW YORK

BROADWAY

Library of Congress Cataloging-in-Publication Data
Cross, Robert G.
Revenue management : hard-core tactics for market
domination / Robert G. Cross.
p. cm.   Includes index.
ISBN 0-553-06734-6
1. Revenue management—United States. I. Title.
HD60.7.C76   1997   658.15′54—dc20
96-32457 CIP

FIRST EDITION

Designed by Julie Duquet

97 98 99 00 10 9 8 7 6 5 4 3 2 1

To my loving wife, Patti, and our children,
Dax, Rebecca, and Zach

And to my parents, Don and Frances Cross

CONTENTS

ACKNOWLEDGMENTS *ix*

INTRODUCTION
COST-CUTTING, REENGINEERING, DOWNSIZING—
NOW WHAT? *1*

CHAPTER
1
ENTROPY, ANOREXIA, AND EMPTY PROFITS *7*

CHAPTER
2
FINDING THE "LOST" $300 MILLION *33*

CHAPTER
3
THE CORE CONCEPTS OF REVENUE
MANAGEMENT *49*

CHAPTER
4
CASE STUDY: THE ATTACK OF THE LASER FARES *99*

CHAPTER

5

THE RM REVOLUTION *131*

CHAPTER

6

LAUNCHING THE REVENUE ROCKET *159*

CHAPTER

7

CASE STUDY: NATIONAL CAR RENTAL'S
NEAR-DEATH EXPERIENCE *191*

CHAPTER

8

WHAT YOU DON'T KNOW ABOUT REVENUE
MANAGEMENT COULD KILL YOU! *215*

CHAPTER

9

THE MARKETING RENAISSANCE *237*

LIST OF INTERVIEWEES *261*

AUTHOR'S NOTE *267*

INDEX *269*

ACKNOWLEDGMENTS

This book is not mine alone. It is a composite of the experiences of a lifetime with a wealth of individuals who have shared their ideas, hopes, disappointments, and achievements.

Much of the conceptual thinking in this book was developed by an incredibly talented group of colleagues at Aeronomics Incorporated. This book reflects their work as much as mine. Over the past twelve years, together we have refined and advanced the art and science of Revenue Management (RM), sharing ideas, testing concepts, overcoming obstacles, and defining the discipline. My initial partners, Steve Swope, Dick Niggley, Ren Curry, Graham Young, Rob Flanegin, and Peter Mahler were true believers from the beginning and have made incalculable contributions to RM and, accordingly, to this book. John Wallace, Tim Hart, Al Payne, Andrew Mace, Loren Williams, Steve Adkins, and Joe Morris have also made tremendous contributions to the success of Revenue Management as an important business discipline. In addition to his significant RM contributions, Larry Hall assumed the responsibility for the daily operation of our company to enable me to focus on developing this book.

A great debt is also owed to the business leaders who had the vision to adopt Revenue Management techniques before they were tested and accepted elsewhere. They are truly innovators who made a major difference. Special thanks goes to the management of Delta Air Lines, particularly Dave Garrett, Ron Allen, Bob Coggin, and Julius Gwin, who were enthusiastic advocates and supporters fourteen years ago when they invested in these revenue-generating concepts, despite intense pressure to reduce costs.

I have also learned a great deal from other business leaders who have been the driving force in the development and adoption of RM concepts in their companies. Bob Crandall of American Airlines can legitimately be referred to as the "Father of Yield Management," and Bill Marriott Jr. pioneered the use of RM in hotels. The indomitable Herb Kelleher of Southwest Airlines and the insightful Sir Colin Marshall of British Airways have also contributed far more to the success of Revenue Management as a fundamental business practice than the credit they receive herein.

Numerous others, many of them Aeronomics' clients, have had great influence on the growth of RM and my work in this area. These include Steve Wolf of United Airlines and USAir, Dr. Alfred Kahn of Cornell University, Gordon Bethune of Continental Airlines, Hollis Harris of Delta Air Lines and Air Canada, Don Burr of PeopleExpress, Dr. Herbert Bammer of Austrian Airlines, Rich Hanks of Marriott International, Paul Noland of Walt Disney World, Tony O'Donovan of IBM, Steve Regulinski of United Airlines, Terry Hardy and Ernest Johnson of National Car Rental System, Graeme Pearce of the International Air Transport Association, Bruce Rowe of Harrah's Casinos, John Koten of Worth Magazine, John Woodley of Morgan Stanley, Cam Fellman of the Television Bureau of Canada, Esther Dyson of Release 1.0, Pat Conroy of Aer Lingus, Kyrl Acton of Lan Chile, Paul Edwards and Will Owens of Qantas Airways, Chris Gibbons of the Promus Companies and Microsoft, Steve Weisz of Marriott International, Dr. Jim Makens of Wake Forest University, Peter Whitford of The Seven Network and others who contributed to this book through interviews, discussions, and other interactions. I have, regretfully, short-changed all their contributions as they have become an inseparable part of my own knowledge and experience.

Tragically, I can no longer thank Carol Meinke, a generous and giving person, whose life was cut short by cancer. Her willingness to experiment with RM concepts in her one-chair barbershop proved that these techniques can be beneficial to virtually any business.

This book would not have been written had it not been for the constant encouragement and guidance of transportation industry expert Dr. Darryl Jenkins, who challenged me to write this book years ago. I am equally indebted to my superb literary agent, Rafe Sagalyn, who believed in these concepts and recognized the need to share them with the larger business community. My publisher, Bill Shinker of Broadway Books, has also been an advocate for this book and a believer in the concepts of RM and their importance to the world of business. My editor, John Sterling, brought focus and clarity to the manuscript. His guidance was invaluable during each phase of the drafting process. Illustrator Scott Price brought creative vision to the text.

I was fortunate to find a number of trusted colleagues at Aeronomics who were willing to review the manuscript drafts and help shape and sharpen the presentation of RM concepts. In particular, I would like to thank Chuck Johnson, an outside director of my company, who thoroughly reviewed each manuscript draft and whose wealth of experience in a variety of industries broadened my perspective and significantly elevated my thinking throughout the process. Of course, nothing could have been accomplished without the dedicated commitment of my right arm, Cindy Taylor. She enabled me to successfully straddle my publishing and consulting commitments over the past four years. I am also grateful to Rich Hanks of Marriott International, Ben Baldanza of Continental Airlines, Bob Collier of InterContinental Hotels and Resorts, business author Tom Petzinger, and Ned Case of NationBank, who reviewed the completed draft and provided insightful comments that were extremely valuable in preparing the final manuscript.

My deepest gratitude goes to Kathy Field, who was brought into the book process when it was little more than an idea. Her original role was in the area of research; however, because of her vast intellectual capabilities, experience, and inexhaustible drive, she played an indispensable role in the development of the book concept, challenging my thinking and greatly influencing the book's structure. Over the past two and a half years, she has become both a collaborator and a dear friend. This book could not have been done without her.

Finally, I must acknowledge the patience and forbearance of my family as I worked through years of information gathering and interviews, then my seclusion during periods of intense manuscript drafting. My wife Patti has been an unwavering and unselfish supporter of this effort and my children believed in the value of what I set out to accomplish. I am truly blessed.

INTRODUCTION

COST-CUTTING, REENGINEERING, DOWNSIZING—NOW WHAT?

In THE TWELVE YEARS since I started my Revenue Management company, I have worked with scores of companies around the world that were looking for ways to deal with today's increasingly chaotic marketplace. Many of these companies were already experiencing urgent financial pressures when they turned to my company for help. Others were preparing to face radical changes in their markets. Most had an acute dread of the unknown—uncertainty was their common enemy.

Some had tried cost-cutting, reengineering, and downsizing with varying degrees of success. These strategies, however, often led to "corporate anorexia," with serious side effects, including killing employee morale and crippling the company's ability to grow. All these companies had to answer to increasingly impatient investors who were not satisfied with squeezing profit out of a shrinking company. Understandably, they were demanding long-term, profitable growth.

But consumers are now more fractious, and competitors, more vicious. When previously successful executives come face-to-face with stubborn problems they have never experienced, their anxiety is acute. Some of the frustrations they have expressed to me may sound familiar:

- "The lousy economy almost killed us, but we got through it. Now, business is finally moving again, and guess what? Our customers are being picked off by these new low-cost guys. We know our stuff is better than theirs. And we service the hell out of our customers. But we're still losing market share."
- "We're working hard. Real hard. We have more customers than ever before. But we're going nowhere on the bottom line—or the top line, for that matter. Look at the last six quarters. Absolutely flat. Nothing is working. This is the worst rut I've ever been in. Frankly, I'm fed up."
- "The good news is that business is picking up. The bad news is that it's only in some markets. Talk about a vicious cycle. Now we've got to spend money to meet new demand in a couple of markets, but the rest of our markets are going nowhere. We've got to get some serious profits, and fast."
- "Our whole industry is sucking wind. We've tried everything we can think of. Nothing seems to work. There's got to be something we're missing. I've never failed before, and I don't intend to start now."

These seasoned executives are savvy businesspeople, but their education and experience did not prepare them for these marketplace predicaments.

Other executives, however, face these same issues and have found a way not only to stay alive but to prosper. They have discovered an array of revenue-enhancing tactics that help them understand their markets better than ever before. They have learned to predict customer demand at the micromarket level and to respond rapidly, as demand changes. They have learned to convert market uncertainty to probability, and probability to profitability. In doing so, they have uncovered the secrets to revenue growth. Using these tactics, some have achieved spectacular results:

- Bob Crandall, who spearheaded the development of these revenue-enhancing tactics at American Airlines, credits them with contributing *$500 million* annually to American.
- The initial use of these tactics at Delta Air Lines yielded over *$300 million* in increased revenue during the first year.
- Bill Marriott Jr. heard about these tactics directly from Crandall. The practice now generates over *$100 million annually* for his hotels.
- Larry Ramaekers, as president of National Car Rental, used these tactics as an integral part of his turnaround strategy at that failing company. In eighteen months, National was pulled from the brink of bankruptcy and transformed into a viable, profitable, revenue-driven firm, *growing at a 20% annual rate.*
- Peter Kretz, general manager of the Canadian Broadcasting Corporation, adopted these tactics and realized a *$2 million gain in the first two weeks.*

These tactics have evolved into a powerful new business discipline now known as Revenue Management (RM), a new way to manage supply and demand. RM is a proven competitive weapon that enables companies to understand the complexities of today's diverse marketplace, deal with them on a micro-market basis, and make decisions confidently and rapidly.

Revenue Management first emerged in the airline industry as a tactic to deal with new low-cost competitors and fierce pricing wars that resulted from deregulation. Now, RM is an essential business practice at all surviving airlines, and RM techniques have been used successfully at hotels, rental car firms, and railroads and are being tested by broadcasters, utilities, manufacturers, cruise lines, and companies in other industries. It's clear that RM can be successfully applied to every kind of business.

Revenue Management is the art and science of predicting real-time customer demand at the micromarket level and optimizing the price and availability of products. The application of RM principles is limitless, and the potential in terms of revenue return is impressive. Firms employing RM techniques have seen revenues increase between 3% and 7% without significant capital expenditures, resulting in a *50% to 100% increase in profits!*

In its most basic form, Revenue Management focuses managers on more keenly observing the buying behavior of customers and making price and product availability adjustments to achieve significant revenue gains. In its high-tech mode, RM is a disciplined process that enables companies to use massive amounts of customer data to dynamically forecast customer behavior at the micromarket level. In all cases, the objective of Revenue Management is to sell the right product to the right customer at the right time for the right price, thereby maximizing revenue from a company's products. RM focuses companies on revenue growth, not cost-cutting and downsizing. It drives bottom-line increases through top-line improvements.

Revenue Management has been the best-kept secret in business for over a decade, but now RM success stories are becoming known and the word is getting out to the broad business audience. The *Wall Street Journal* recently called Revenue Management an emerging business strategy that is "poised to explode."

Revenue Management: Hard-core Tactics for Market Domination reveals secrets that are critical for long-term success in a chaotic marketplace, such as how to

- Discount with discretion to build market share
- Uncover hidden demand which allows opportunistic pricing
- Understand consumer tradeoffs between price and other product attributes
- Increase revenue without increasing products or promotions
- Identify "lost" revenue opportunity
- Use market intelligence as a competitive weapon
- Establish a revenue-driven organization focusing on profitable growth

As word of RM successes has spread, business executives have increasingly asked me where they can find comprehensive information about this new strategy. Unfortunately, the available published material has been limited to a few articles in specialized trade magazines and academic papers, none of which provide a high-level discussion of RM techniques or answer basic questions about how RM can apply to a range of businesses. I wrote *Revenue Management: Hard-core Tactics for Market Domination* to address these needs.

I hope this book will encourage executives who are faced with market turmoil to focus on solutions that address the *external* market, rather than relying solely on *internal* actions like downsizing. Shrinking a company is sometimes necessary, but it's not the way to ensure long-term profitability. Growth comes from the marketplace, not the workplace. The key to real growth is learning how to deal effectively and proactively with a constantly changing market. That's what Revenue Management is all about.

ENTROPY, ANOREXIA, AND EMPTY PROFITS

It's like we came into the office one day and they told us that everything we had been doing for years was suddenly irrelevant. The insecurity got so bad that no one could concentrate on doing any work. Anyway, by this time, we weren't sure what work we were supposed to be doing or how we were supposed to be doing it. Management went into a shell and wouldn't listen to our ideas. It was very confusing, and everyone was scared. People were leaving every day, and we were all waiting for the ax to fall.

—DOWNSIZING AS DESCRIBED BY ONE OF ITS VICTIMS

MISSING THE BUS

THE GROWING UNCERTAINTY in business is all around us. It's impossible to ignore. Every time I open the *Wall Street Journal, Business Week, Fortune, Forbes,* or other business publications these days, I find an abundance of stories about companies struggling with change. Some strategies adopted by management today are clearly causing more problems than they are solving. Take the story of Greyhound Bus Lines, for example.

Greyhound had sailed along for decades as the dominant player in its industry. Then came the explosive 1980s—competition from left field, defecting customers, strikes by frustrated employees, disgruntled shareholders, a leveraged buyout, red ink, and a trip to bankruptcy court. Then, more changes—restructuring, hiring a dynamic new management team, downsizing, reengineering everything in sight, lopping off $100 million in expenses, reducing the fleet by 50%, cutting labor by 20%, jettisoning high-cost, long-term employees and hiring low-cost part-timers and new recruits. And all of this took place in just a couple of years!

Things began to look up—cost-cutting produced the first profit in years; an exciting "state of the art" computer system promised to automate inventory (bus seats), organize customer transactions, and provide up-to-date information for operational planning; a new 800 telephone number was installed to give greater access to customers. Wall Street applauded, praised the turnaround team, and traded the newly issued stock at twice the value the team expected. A classic turnaround story of the 1990s, right?

Wrong. In reality, Greyhound was playing a game of corporate jeopardy and losing. The company thought they had all the right answers—after all, scores of companies were following the same basic strategies. The problem was that the questions were all wrong. Greyhound was missing the bus big time, and Wall Street was missing the bus right along with it.

In short order, the transitory profits from cost-cutting and downsizing dissolved into a sea of red ink. An unforgiving taskmaster, Wall Street reacted swiftly and certainly. Stock prices plunged, investors were furious, the CEO was forced out, management was accused of misconduct and deceit, and investors threatened another bankruptcy proceeding. Then came more financial restructuring, more downsizing, and frantic efforts to make the "computer system from hell" work in a desperate attempt to keep the company alive.

These strategies only made things worse. Greyhound did nothing to address consumers' needs, and its natural market continued to erode as nontraditional competition from low-cost airlines moved in. Investors ran out of patience. Despite spending a reported $6 million on new computer technology, the company still did not have the basic information needed to understand its customers and respond to their needs. Today Greyhound is still alive, but it's still struggling.

ENTROPY

Unfortunately, Greyhound is not an isolated case. In my work, I see many companies experiencing some of the same problems that hit Greyhound. All are being affected by the greatest unseen challenge facing today's business manager: entropy.

Entropy is the scientific term for the amount of energy unavailable for useful work. This measure of the amount of disorder in processes and systems was first described by the German physicist Rudolf Clausius in 1865. Like gravity, acceleration, and magnetism, entropy is a readily observable phenomenon, and it is affecting our personal and business lives in a very real way.

It is a fundamental principle of physics that entropy relentlessly increases over time; it is difficult, if not impossible, to reverse. For example, it is easier to scramble an egg than to unscramble it; it is easier to shuffle a deck of cards than to re-sort it into its original numerical order. Things left to themselves will move to a higher state of entropy. Just look at the disorder your house and car will fall into if left to themselves.

Most businesses don't understand the concept of entropy, so they haven't yet formulated a way to deal with it. We readily use other concepts from physics in business every day. Everyone knows, for instance, what the terms *momentum* and *acceleration* mean in business. But use of the term *entropy* is not widespread, even though the phenomenon of entropy is clearly happening. In fact, its impact is growing to the point that we can no longer ignore it. More important, we cannot fail to deal with it. Here's why:

- The basic principles of entropy hold in business, just as in physics. The amount of entropy (disorder) in business is increasing with time.
- Randomness and disorder in business will continue to increase.
- Unchecked disorder will result in death by entropy, where chaos reigns.

The signs of increasing entropy are all around us. Corporations are coming and going faster than ever before. CEOs don't last as long as they used to. Consumer products are being introduced and withdrawn more rapidly than in the past. Every day, businesspeople are faced with more information, choices, and issues, all of which have to be dealt with in increasingly less time. In every segment of the marketplace, disorder and fragmentation are rapidly replacing order and homogeneity.

Greyhound's story illustrates a critical point: there are two types of entropy affecting business—*internal entropy,* which is characterized by the expenditure of unproductive energy within an organization, and *external entropy,* which is associated with disorder and chaos in the marketplace. The combination of external entropy in Greyhound's market and internal entropy from Greyhound's "turnaround" activity delivered a devastating double whammy. Entropy was threatening to kill Greyhound. Even so, Wall Street got caught up in the turnaround effort and didn't recognize the real dangers because the "formula" looked right.

Internal entropy is created by people within an organization who are focused on the wrong issues; this in turn renders that energy unavailable for useful work. Every company should strive to be efficient, and cost restructuring may be required to ensure survival in some instances. But cost-cutting is a short-term tactic. In the long term, cost-cutting can lead to "corporate anorexia," a term coined by Gary Hamel and C. K. Prahalad in their book, *Competing for the Future,* to describe companies that cut costs and employees until they are so weak they are unable to grow.

While corporate anorexia may produce apparent short-term transitory profits, cuts in R&D, marketing, sales, and information technology often improve the current quarter's bottom line at the expense of long-term growth and profitability. Successive waves of slash-and-burn tactics tend to increase uncertainty in the workforce and divert people from productive work. Worried employees talk to coworkers about job concerns, thereby spreading stress and entropy throughout the company. Gradually, investors are discovering that these short-term gains are empty profits—illusory benefits of corporate anorexia.

External entropy is the disorder caused by outside forces that affect companies but cannot be directly controlled, such as consumer attitudes, new competition, competitive actions, technological advances, geopolitical factors, economic gyrations, and cataclysmic events. Corporate-centric companies often make the mistake of using internal downsizing and cost-cutting as their primary response to changes in their external business environment.

Larry Ramaekers, former president of National Car Rental

and now a consultant specializing in turning around troubled companies, knows all about external entropy. After working at a brewery and a soft-drink bottler, Ramaekers started his own business. "I bought a soft-drink bottling business in Saginaw, Michigan, and did okay until 1981," he recalls. "Then, Saginaw fell off the face of the earth because of the automobile downturn, and my customers were all laid off. Under these circumstances, soft drinks are something people can do without. At the same time, interest rates went up to 20.5%. I lost my ass."

External entropy is rapidly increasing and is irreversible. The signs are everywhere: customers are more fickle and unpredictable than ever before. The market is getting more crowded with new competitors. Uncertainty about the future is escalating. Change is happening fast, and everything is becoming ever more chaotic and disordered. Every aspect of corporate existence is affected by growing entropy. Things that were stable are now unstable. Things that were certain are now uncertain. The pillars that have supported companies for decades have been seriously undermined. Future shock has arrived.

FOUR FRACTURED PILLARS

In my work with a wide range of companies, I've identified four major areas where disorder has shaken many businesses to their foundation: consumers, investors, the business environment, and information technology. Only by understanding the dramatic changes in these areas and their impact on business can managers begin to devise new strategies for survival.

NONCONFORMIST CONSUMERS

Consumers are restless. Armed with an abundance of information about a universe of options, they are demanding faster, better, and cheaper alternatives. They want—and can get—goods and services that appeal to their individual tastes. From designer jeans to designer pizza to designer condoms, consumer markets are becoming more fragmented, disordered, and chaotic.

Brand loyalty has become somewhat of an oxymoron. In the past, people used branded products to reflect how they wanted to be defined by others. In the beer market, brands like Budweiser and Miller Lite were built on consumer desire to identify with jovial jocks. Consumers wanted to be part of the mass market of winners. What beer you drank and what car you drove defined to others who you were. Today, people more often refuse to be defined, classified, or pigeonholed. They revel in their diversity.

Today's nonconformist consumers are ambivalent about designating a specific brand of beer as a status symbol. They are brand independent and proud of it. They want to try them all. To appease these consumers, the beer industry has come alive with choice: light beers, dry beers, ice beers, clear beers, nonalcoholic beers, ales, lagers, pilsners, stouts, bitters, and bocks. The production of microbreweries quintupled between 1990 and 1994. Anheuser-Busch created a "Specialty Brews Group" to respond to further market fragmentation and to develop new brews like Red Wolf Lager and Elk Mountain Ale to compete for diverse consumer tastes.

On a recent flight from Asia to the United States, I met a young entrepreneur who was planning to import beer from Nepal to take advantage of this market fragmentation. "Is this stuff any good?" I asked, skeptical about Nepalese beer. "Not really," he answered candidly. So why was he hauling cases of this so-so stuff back to the land of free-flowing beer? He figured he could make a lot of money from one-time buyers willing to pay a premium price to try something different.

Entropy has killed the mass market and replaced it with what I call "amoeba markets." Amoeba markets constantly change shape and subdivide, fragmenting into smaller micromarkets at ever faster rates. The only thing you can say collectively about consumers today is that they represent a market that is increasingly chaotic. Dieter Huckestein, president of the hotel division at Hilton Hotels Corporation, calls this phenomenon "the new world disorder."

Just look at what's happening in television—mecca for the mass market. For decades, three networks dominated the U.S. airwaves. They had unique commercial power to broadcast product messages to a mass market. The amoeba market changed all that. Now, broadcasting is out, narrowcasting is in. The average U.S. household now has thirty to fifty channels, with new customized channels being added at a staggering rate. But not even these customized channels can hold the attention of fidgety viewers who are constantly channel surfing.

Market fragmentation is seen in virtually every consumer market. In 1994, over twenty thousand new consumer products were launched—almost fifteen times as many as in 1970, when only about fourteen hundred new products were launched. Most of the new products are variants of existing products (e.g., different flavors, colors, and sizes) designed to appeal to individual tastes of nonconformist consumers comprising a growing number of micromarkets.

Today's consumers demand to be treated as individuals. And, as collections of individuals, they are wielding more power than they did in the days of the traditional mass market. They are demanding customized products. Marketers are getting the message and are looking for niches that will produce sustainable profits from product tailoring.

Nudists, for example, have become a profitable niche for travel companies. The American Association for Nude Recreation claims forty-six-thousand members with impressive demographics: 47% earn more than $50,000 a year, and 77% are college educated. Some cruise lines have tailored the cruise experience for this niche, and the first "clothing optional" cruise was launched in 1992. Now, nude cruises routinely sail at 100% capacity and sell out months in advance, contrasting with the average 75% occupancy on regular sailings.

Companies with the ability to anticipate consumer demand and preferences will be the successful marketers of the next century. The challenge is how to develop this ability in an environment of increasing entropy in consumer markets and attitudes. The new consumer is eluding traditional market research methods. In 1992, companies reportedly paid a record $5 billion to the fifty largest research firms to learn more about their customers. That same year, an estimated 83% of new products failed to produce minimum acceptable launch results.

These nonconformist groups of consumers are skeptical, capricious, and rebellious—and getting more so. They are more tactical in their purchase decisions and are willing to alter buying patterns on relatively small differentials in price, product, or delivery.

Price, especially, matters more than ever. Price promotions, private labels, and the rise of megadiscount stores such as Circuit City, Sam's Club, and OfficeMax have kept the discount message in front of consumers. Even luxury item providers—such as automakers Mercedes Benz and BMW, luxury hotels, and cruise lines—haven't escaped the new price/value mentality. They too have had to develop discount products to satisfy consumer demands.

THE SUMMER OF '95—DISCOUNTS IN ALL THE RIGHT PLACES

Four Seasons Hotels	30%–50% off
Ritz-Carlton Hotels	Up to 50% off
Grand Hyatt Hotels	Up to 50% off
Queen Odyssey Luxury Cruise Line	Two-for-one on two-week cruise
QE II	50% off

The discount mentality shows no signs of reversing. According to *Roper's Public Pulse,* more people now than at any time in the last twenty years say that reasonable price is their top purchase criteria, rivaling quality.

But consumers are also demanding value. They want the best possible product at the best possible price with the best possible service. They will trade features for price and price for service. The consumer seeks instant gratification to fulfill a current need. Consumer attitudes change depending on the particular circumstances of time and place. For a new water heater in the dead of winter, brand and price might take a back seat to fast delivery; in the middle of a long, hot summer, the urgency for a water heater may not be so great. Then, product feature and price might be more important.

The tough new consumer demands a customized blend of product, service, and price—right now! These requirements change based on factors you can't control, but you have to deliver, because if you don't, someone else will. As Dieter

Huckestein puts it, "The customer is in charge in this new world disorder, and we all know that customers vote with their feet."

The Nonconformist Consumer

- Has seized market power from companies
- Refuses to be classified
- Demands instant gratification
- Wants lots of options
- Demands value—trading off price, quality, and convenience

ACTIVIST INVESTORS

Descriptions of today's tough new consumer—demanding, impatient, independent, restless—are the same for today's tough new "activist" investor. Dealing with shareholders used to be simple. Managers managed while shareholders collected dividends. As a rule, shareholders stayed in the background and were quiet and cordial at shareholder meetings. Even when the majority of shareholdings shifted from individuals to institutions, shares in a company were typically passive investments. If the company did not live up to shareholder expectations, investors simply sold their stock. They devoted their energies to picking stocks, not running the company. No more.

Like consumers, investors are no longer passive. They are exerting power as owners, closely monitoring management decisions. They are asking tough questions at shareholder meetings and are challenging executive salaries and corporate perks. Some of them are running for directorships. Investors are becoming increasingly impatient and dissatisfied, even with good results. They want it all and they want it *now*.

Today's CEO is on a short leash that is increasingly being yanked by investors. CEOs of companies performing below investors' expectations wait for the ax to fall. It makes no difference if they are strong managers doing a great job under difficult circumstances beyond their control. Bottom-line performance that increases stock value is what counts, not effort. In the investor's view, when bottom-line performance isn't there it was the CEO who screwed up. In the past five years, the heads of well-known CEOs have rolled at an unprecedented rate. Gone are John Akers from IBM, Robert Stempel from GM, and James Robinson from American Express.

Even CEOs who have produced years of profits are not immune from investor scrutiny. ITT's Rand Araskog, for example, produced an annual rate of return of over 11.5% during the first five years of the 1990s, when the ROI at many companies deteriorated. Nonetheless, the Pension Fund of the International Brotherhood of Teamsters didn't want to leave the decision making for deals like ITT's acquisition of lodging/gaming company Caesar's World in the hands of Araskog alone. They wanted to validate the chairman's plans.

Institutional fund managers are turning up the heat on companies in which their funds hold significant positions, giving rise to a new breed of consultant-lobbyists who study the relationship between executive performance and compensation and who pressure directors to eliminate excessive perks. The fund managers are asking pointed questions at annual meetings and refuse to accept vague answers, putting CEOs on notice that the institutional investor is watching every move. Before, CEOs could count on a couple of years to learn the business and develop a plan. Now, investors are looking for immediate action. They want instant improvement.

Investors are also determining that profits resulting from cost-cutting and downsizing may be short-term empty profits that don't reflect the company's future potential in an increasingly uncertain and fiercely competitive marketplace. The stock market regularly delivers blunt messages to this effect, and, as many companies are finding out, Wall Street is a mercurial place.

The recent history of IBM is a case in point. In January 1995, IBM reported that its fourth-quarter 1994 profits had tripled over those of the previous year's quarter—from $382 million to a whopping $1.2 billion. The results for the year were even better. In 1994 IBM earned $3 billion, compared with $148 million in 1993. You'd think that IBM stock would show a healthy gain for such an earnings achievement, but Wall Street reacted negatively to IBM's results, driving down the stock price 1⅛ a share. In the recent past, when institutional and mutual fund managers took the bottom line at face value, IBM stock would have been snapped up. But another number caught the attention of the new activist investors: annual revenue growth. In 1994, IBM's worldwide revenues were flat, growing by only 2.1%. Wall Street expressed major concern over this number. IBM's CFO responded with a general statement indicating that IBM was focusing on stronger revenue growth but conceded that IBM didn't know how fast it could grow.

Just a couple of months after this apparently bleak situation, IBM reported that first-quarter 1995 revenues rose to $15.7 billion, an 18% improvement over the first quarter of 1994. Earnings were $1.29 billion, a threefold increase from the 1994 quarter's $392 million. This time, Wall Street was ecstatic. IBM shares were traded in unusually large volume, and the price rose 1⅞ a share.

THE ACTIVIST INVESTOR

- Wants instant gratification and demands immediate results
- Values stock appreciation often more than dividends
- Has instant access to detailed financial information via computer
- Does not passively accept a "bad investment" decision
- Demands performance from executives (or heads will roll)

THE UNSTABLE BUSINESS ENVIRONMENT

When Ray Kroc, the fast-food king who built McDonald's Corporation, was asked what he would do if a competitor was drowning, Kroc didn't hesitate. "Put a hose in his mouth," he replied. Kroc understood that business is war.

Gen. A. M. Gray, former commandant of the U.S. Marine Corps, describes the fluid nature of war in his book, *Warfighting*. "Success," he says, "will depend on the continuing ability to adapt to the constantly changing situation." So it is with business, where the only constant is constant uncertainty. Business, like armed conflict, takes place in what General Gray calls "the fog of war." Companies will always have inexact, incomplete, and contradictory information about the market and competition. Yet they must use the information they have to develop a plan of action. As companies do battle, disorder escalates. Plans go awry, instructions are misinterpreted, "stealth" competitors sneak in, and unforeseen events become commonplace. Increasingly, winning depends on your ability to deal with this escalating disorder better than your competitors.

Not so long ago, the corner druggist knew that his competition was the drugstore across the street. The friction generated by that competition was relatively easy to overcome. The druggist, who was also typically the owner, had the essential information about his competitor to compete effectively, and neither competitor wanted a deadly clash. Now the battle lines are unclear. Stealth competitors exist. Who exactly is the enemy? The local druggist is besieged. Pharmaceuticals are sold by large chains of drugstores, supermarkets, megastores, clinics, and mail order houses. Some companies don't have a clue who their current competitors (never mind future ones) really are.

In the case of Greyhound, other bus companies didn't steal market share, automakers and discount airlines did. Customer stealing used to take place almost exclusively in price wars between like-product competitors or in improved product offerings from like-product competitors. Now, competition is coming from sources no one would have ever imagined a decade ago. Competitors used to be local; now they are global. Indirect competition is growing rapidly. Competition from substitutable commodities, new technologies, new sources of supply, and service add-ons can be impossible to anticipate in advance. It's difficult to fight unknown enemies.

Other extreme changes are occurring in the business environment as well. Globalization, freer trade, privatization, and deregulation will all have far-reaching, radical effects. They will create fear for some, opportunity for others.

The deregulation of electric power utilities is a case in point. Deregulation will tear down long-protected markets and margins, threatening high-cost electricity producers, some of whom are saddled with billions of dollars in debt from nuclear plants, which they expected to pay for from rising consumer rates. This will create a familiar vicious circle: when customers abandon high-cost suppliers, these suppliers raise their rates to the remaining customers to cover fixed costs, which in turn drives more customers away, until bankruptcy becomes a very real threat.

Deregulation shock waves are affecting huge industries, including banking, trucking, railroads, broadcasting, electric utilities, gas utilities, and telecommunications. Companies in these industries have to learn how to deal with the amoeba market—a complex and hostile environment with demanding consumers, disgruntled investors, ruthless competitors, accelerating change, and an uncertain future. In other words, they will have to deal with the real world.

THE UNSTABLE BUSINESS ENVIRONMENT

- Disorder in the marketplace increases rapidly.
- Intangibles such as speed, flexibility, responsiveness, adaptability, and quality are driving businesses.
- Unknown "stealth" competitors replace known, local competitors.
- Competition intensifies.

THE INFORMATION EXPLOSION

Information is power. In corporate wars, winning and losing often depend on the quality of available information. Companies must be able to read the competitive situation and respond quickly. However, risk is inherent in the decision-making process. No decision in business today can be made with 100% certainty. But we all know that this element of risk is what makes the job of management so exciting. Calling the right shots in tough situations is exhilarating, but get it wrong and you're dead. Despite all the talk from management gurus about encouraging "creative failure," investors are coldly intolerant of managers' mistakes that negatively affect the value of their holdings.

The accuracy and completeness of information reduces the risk in decision making. Unfortunately, though, information is subject to the ravages of entropy. Each transmission of information distorts the original message. Every successive communication of data adds more noise or omits details, further distorting the initial data.

Conscious biases can distort the information base in a corporate environment and lead to greater entropy. We've all known people who exaggerate a situation to make a point or use "selective memory" to reach a decision they are predisposed to make. Unintentional biases also distort the information used to make decisions. My colleague, Dr. Ren Curry, has studied unintentional biases and learned a great deal about the ways humans consistently misinterpret data or make incorrect suppositions about the data. Unfortunately, these suppositions often become part of the corporate body of knowledge.

A quick look at some of these unintentional biases illustrates the problem. The "availability bias," for instance, describes how people inadvertently consider information more important if it is readily available or easier to recall. Something happening today is given more weight than something, perhaps more relevant, that happened last week. Another unintentional bias is called "order effects," which occur when people unintentionally give undue importance to the first and last items in a series. Job interviews and sales calls in the middle of a series have to be extraordinary to compensate for this disadvantageous position.

Critical decisions are made every day on the wrong information, biased information, or information that is so superficial that it does not represent a true picture of the facts. Reports and statistics can be slanted to reflect a particular point of view, so decisions may not be made on what the important factors really are but on what someone else thinks they are. Data is another major issue. How is data collected at the point of sale? What happens when the data is bad? What happens when the information compiled from the data is sketchy, incomplete, or just plain wrong?

The problems inherent in information-based decision making are compounded by the rapid employee turnover in companies. Years ago, managers worked their way up in a single organization and knew a lot about the market from personal observation. As the market grew and these managers increasingly relied on data from the field, they knew the data collection method and understood what the data represented. Data distortion and misinterpretation were less likely. By 1991, however, nearly one out of every three U.S. workers had been with their employer less than a year. The corporate penchant for downsizing is accelerating this trend. Managers are now likely to spend their career working for several companies. More often than not, they have to rely on reports and statistics without understanding the source or nature of the data and statistical calculations on which their business decisions are made.

Staying afloat in the swelling seas of information is also a growing challenge. The amount of information available today is staggering and is growing at a phenomenal rate. More information has been produced in the last thirty years than in the previous five thousand. A single copy of today's *New York Times* weekday edition contains more information than a person in the seventeenth century was likely to encounter in a lifetime.

In business, the amount of information available to managers also is growing exponentially. Information technology is now the most rapidly growing segment of the economy. Of the $52 billion to be spent on reengineering projects in the near future, $42 billion will be spent on associated information systems. Information is ruling our lives. Now, one of our greatest challenges is learning how to rule information. That's why a larger percentage of corporate budgets is allocated to information technology these days.

The mission behind all these efforts to improve information technology is to find a way to deal with the escalating need for speed and accuracy in the decision-making process. The speed of a decision may be as critical as the decision itself. A good decision now might be worth more than a great decision later. Superior speed and accurate decision making allow companies to take the initiative, dictate the terms of competition, and force competitors to be reactionary. That's why critical mass is being replaced by critical speed as an essential corporate attribute. The observation of Sun-tzu in 400 B.C. that "speed is the essence of war" has tremendous validity in today's business world.

The need for greater accuracy with greater speed is making

the development of information systems more ambitious, more complex, and much riskier. Over 30% of major information system developments fail, and a failed systems project can wreak havoc on a company. One mortgage company was forced into Chapter 11 bankruptcy when a $20 million computer systems project ballooned into a $100 million-plus nightmare. Coincidentally, the debt figure used at the bankruptcy proceeding was exactly $100 million.

Intelligent sorting and filtering of growing stores of information is the real value for companies. It is more critical than ever to get the right information to the right manager at the right time for the right decision to be made quickly. The manipulation and sharing of appropriate information is one of the biggest issues facing companies today. Get it right, and you move fast and win. Get it wrong, and you've created destructive internal entropy.

THE INFORMATION EXPLOSION

- The amount of information available to decision makers is doubling every seven years.
- Information will replace tangibles as a company's most important asset.
- To win in the rapidly evolving marketplace, more information must be transmitted and shared more frequently.
- Each transmission of data can increase distortion and confusion.
- Information overload and misinterpretation can create deadly internal entropy.

TROUBLE IN GURULAND

Dealing effectively with the chaos and uncertainty of today's marketplace should be at the top of corporate agendas everywhere. It is not surprising that there is plenty of advice for executives. In recent years, management gurus have come up with an alphabet soup of managerial techniques—JIT (just-in-time), TQC (total quality control), SPC (statistical process control), TQM (total quality management), and BPR (business process reengineering), to name a few. Most of these techniques offer ideas that have a great deal of merit, but many companies are having trouble translating these management concepts into solutions that work on a long-term basis.

The philosophy of total quality management, for instance, has been widely credited with transforming "made in Japan" from a joke into a standard for excellence. The theory is that if you get the processes right, high-quality products will be produced at the lowest possible cost and this will ensure success in the marketplace. But, like many philosophies, there's a major difference between thinking it and doing it, not to mention doing it right. Only about 30% of the five hundred U.S. companies surveyed in 1992 by Arthur D. Little thought their TQM programs had significant impact on their competitive position.

Take reengineering, an exciting concept that offers a great deal of promise but few notable success stories. The underlying theory is fundamentally sound: most companies operate under a jumble of jerry-built internal processes designed for a simpler time and they don't make sense in today's rapidly evolving environment. Reengineering promises a quantum leap in performance through radical redesign of a company's processes, organization, and culture. Some reengineered corporations have saved hundreds of millions of dollars a year. Many reengineering efforts, however, haven't contributed a single penny to the bottom line, yet they have boosted costs and created internal entropy.

In 1994, U.S. companies reportedly spent $32 billion on reengineering programs. That figure is expected to increase to $52 billion by 1997, with $40 billion or so going to information systems (according to a survey of twelve hundred corporations by *Systems Reengineering Economics,* a newsletter published by Computer Economics Inc.).

Michael Hammer, coauthor of *Reengineering the Corporation,* says that approximately 70% of the projects labeled "reengineering" are failing, indicating that the companies either don't understand the nature of reengineering or don't have the commitment and leadership of top management. Coauthor James Champy's CSC Index Consulting firm surveyed six hundred senior managers and found that 69% of North American companies surveyed conducted one or more reengineering projects. Of this group, 16% reported extraordinary results, 17% reported strong results, and 67% reported disappointing results. More than 40% of the disappointed managers reported mediocre to marginal results, and 25% said that the programs failed outright. Citibank N.A. admitted that its year-long $50 million attempt to reengineer the processing of securities was a fiasco.

Why have companies failed to see significant benefits from reengineering efforts? Perhaps making radical changes in large organizations is a more complex task than they thought. Additionally, there is no established scientific formula or disciplined process to accomplish reengineering. Reengineering is essentially a philosophy that can be applied in thousands of different ways and can address thousands of different work processes. If companies select the wrong process to reengineer or go about it in the wrong way, they can end up wasting a great deal of time and money.

Downsizing, also referred to as "neutron-bomb reengineering," is the harsh business of cutting costs by sacking people in an attempt to get productivity increases. Downsizing could legitimately be called a craze in the United States, with almost three-quarters of the companies surveyed by Right Associates, a Philadelphia-based consulting firm, admitting to doing it over the last five years. According to the study, all this slashing and cutting did not result in much gain. Three-quarters of the downsizing firms said that they saw no financial improvement as a result. Over 65% said they had not seen any improvement in productivity. They did, however, experience confusion and disorder in the workplace. When jobs are cut, the work is seldom reduced proportionally, leaving overworked and insecure survivors to pick up the slack. It's not easy to raise productivity when morale is slumping.

Further complicating this troubled situation is that some of the gurus' advice appears contradictory. TQM is a doctrine of continuous, incremental improvement; BPR stresses throwing out the old and starting fresh. TQM emphasizes the value of the individual employee; BPR wants to squeeze more out of fewer employees and resources. Still, some desperate companies try to employ them simultaneously. As the marketplace becomes ever more difficult, companies are desperately seeking solutions. As the *Economist* described it, "The world is full of ailing firms flitting between fads." There is plenty more advice out there. Business books, offering all manner of theoretical solutions, represent one of the fastest-growing segments in the publishing industry, but few seem to be offering substantive solutions, let alone ways to achieve long-term success. Much of the advice reads like pop psychology. Business leaders are told to pursue "wow" and to "zap" their way to success. How do you deal with increasing external entropy? Try "thriving on chaos" or "creating a crazy organization." I'm not suggesting that these management theories have no value. In fact, some of them may be essential to success. It depends on what your problems are. A stale, lethargic company should seek motivation and inspiration. Bloated and inefficient businesses should consider reengineering and perhaps an intelligent approach to downsizing. Unfocused companies should seek vision, purpose, and direction.

The problem is that most of the suggestions from the gurus are internally focused and corporate-centric. They deal with *your* processes, *your* organization, *your* management style. But what if your real problem is external? What if it is the increasing fragmentation of your customer base? What if it is competition from left field? You can be running a lean machine today and be history tomorrow if you are not selling the right product to the right customer at the right time for the right price.

As the promise of reengineering and downsizing fades, it's time for a completely new approach.

REFRAMING THE ISSUES

For centuries, people believed that the earth was the center of the universe. It seemed obvious to the naked eye that the earth remained motionless while the sun, moon, and stars revolved around it. In the early sixteenth century, however, Copernicus reframed the question and came to a different conclusion. Employing a broader perspective and an open mind, he liberated himself from conventional wisdom and discovered that all the planets in the solar system, including the earth, revolved around the sun.

Similarly, companies today must liberate themselves from traditional perspectives and reframe the issues facing them in an increasingly entropic marketplace. Investors are no longer interested in profitable but shrinking companies. They are looking for growth. But growth is not easy to deliver on a sustained basis in today's amoeba market.

"Brilliant" corporate strategies no longer ensure success in this rapidly moving, increasingly disordered world. Nor does the conventional wisdom of today's management gurus sufficiently address external market issues now facing companies. Cost control and continued productivity increases in the workplace are essential for long-term survival, but you can't cost-cut your way to prosperity. Prosperity comes only from real growth. And real growth comes only from the marketplace.

To achieve sustainable growth, companies must adopt a much broader perspective. They must become less corporate-centric and more market-centric. The market, not the company, must become the center of the universe. For the past decade, too many companies have been concentrating on internal cost-cutting processes. It's time to focus on the external market and the revenue side of the profit equation.

This shift in emphasis poses a number of important questions. How can you focus on increasing revenue production from your existing asset base and product set? How can you—whether you market products or services—address non-conformist consumers one at a time? How can you understand an individual customer's unique requirements and willingness to pay? *Most important, how can you maximize your revenues on each and every sale?*

The answers to these questions are found in Revenue Management techniques. RM enhances revenue productivity by achieving a precise understanding of the demand for a company's products and services at the micromarket level. It requires a dynamic reassessment of the marketplace to ensure that a company's revenues are maximized by optimizing the price and availability of its products. It requires that managers focus on revenue generation, not just cost control, and turn their attention to top-line techniques to drive bottom-line results.

Revenue Management casts a business in a whole new light. Instead of asking how much productivity can be squeezed from people and processes, the question becomes "How much revenue can we generate from the marketplace with our existing resources?"

RM can be applied at any level in a variety of businesses, from small shops to multibillion-dollar international corporations. Part of what makes it so powerful is attitude—Revenue Management is a single-minded effort to search out revenue opportunities that may not be readily apparent to others. In its most sophisticated form, RM is an exciting marriage of marketing and technology, employing rocket science mathematics. The hard-core tactics of Revenue Management focus a company on revenue growth. They help your company understand consumer tradeoffs and achieve market domination.

FINDING THE "LOST" $300 MILLION

*You cannot risk creating the impression that you are the
high-priced product in the marketplace. You've always
got to be competitive to some degree.*
—ROBERT COGGIN, EXECUTIVE VICE PRESIDENT,
DELTA AIR LINES, INC.

THE MOTHER OF INVENTION

FOR OVER A DECADE, MY
Revenue Management company, Aeronomics, has helped
some of the best-known companies around the world to use
RM techniques to increase their revenues. My company has
also done a considerable amount of work developing the art
and science of Revenue Management. But I didn't set out to
build a career or a company based on Revenue Management.
As a lawyer, my career goal was to advance in the practice of
law and eventually obtain a judgeship. My introduction to the
powerful concepts behind RM was a happenstance that I
could not have possibly anticipated.

Following a stint as general counsel of the Texas Aeronautics Commission, I accepted a position in the law department of Delta Air Lines, just as the deregulation of the U.S. airline industry was starting to unfold. Delta had a unique corporate culture and had historically marched to the beat of its own drum. It had always been a strong company, a real winner. This fierce individualism paid off in impressive profits year after year. For decades, Delta was the most consistently profitable airline in the highly leveraged airline industry. This record was unmatched by any other airline and was a major source of pride for every Delta employee.

Following the passage of the Airline Deregulation Act in the late 1970s, the U.S. airline industry was in great disarray and the market was going crazy. The airlines had operated for forty years with federal regulators telling them where they could fly and what they could charge. Now they could do whatever they wanted, whenever they wanted, and charge whatever the market would bear. Freed from restrictive government shackles, some of them went berserk. They bought tons of new planes, started up new routes left and right, and slashed fares to grab market share in a hurry. It didn't take long for their debt to pile up.

Established airlines like American, United, PanAm, TWA, Northwest, and Delta struggled to understand what was happening. New, low-cost airlines, such as PeopleExpress, were born, coming to the market with a different strategy. They bought cheap, used airplanes and operated with low-seniority, low-wage workers. Their costs were about half those of the established major airlines. It didn't take long before they were stealing market share.

With aggressive new competitors suddenly entering the fray, all-out war was inevitable. The low-fare airlines attacked the markets previously "owned" by established airlines, and established airlines invaded each other's turf. Fares plunged as the fighting got more intense. It seemed like no one was acting rationally—except Delta.

At Delta, we were determined to stick to our conservative growth plan. We resisted the drastic discounting and concentrated on our reputation as a business travelers' airline with a superior product. However, we could not ignore that we were being invaded everywhere. The lucrative Northeast-to-Florida markets we had owned for years were under attack by the discounters. Business travelers were beginning to defect to the cheap-fare airlines as well. No markets were "ours" anymore.

Delta's strong record of profits began to erode. The elements that had made Delta so successful in the past—on-time performance, friendly customer service, and efficient operations—were no longer providing the competitive edge in the new amoeba market. Senior management started looking for people who could provide a fresh, new perspective. They felt that someone outside the traditional marketing role could look at things more objectively and might be able to see what we were missing.

Marketing was the last place I expected to find myself. But after working on strategies to deal with the fuel crisis of the early 1980s, I came to the attention of senior management and was invited to join the marketing division in a new, free-form position designed to identify problems and new opportunities on the marketing side. Basically, it was an internal consulting job with no direct responsibility but lots of apparent authority. I thought it would be an interesting sidebar to my legal career for a couple of years. The judgeship could wait for a while.

Soon after I started in marketing, I was invited to a major strategy meeting. It was clear that we would have to get down and dirty in the fare wars if we were going to win. Out of that meeting came an advertising campaign in which Delta declared it would "meet or beat" everyone's fares on competitive routes. We had to reverse the momentum of the market, refocus attention on Delta, and dispel the notion that Delta was high-priced and noncompetitive.

The response was fantastic. The public loved it. Phones rang off the hooks in the reservations department. People lined up at Delta ticket counters all over the country to take advantage of this offer. We carried more passengers than ever before in Delta's history, and we worked harder than ever. Reservations and airport people worked overtime to meet the demand. *But we still lost our shirts.* "Meet or Beat" produced loads of passenger traffic, but the fares were so low we couldn't make money on many of our flights even if they went out completely full. "Meet or Beat" reversed traffic losses, but it wasn't the answer. In effect, we had put our competitors and the advertising agency in charge of our pricing.

At the close of that fiscal year, Delta reported its first annual loss in thirty-six years. Shock reverberated throughout the company. Most employees had never seen red ink in their entire Delta careers. With record numbers of passengers, they were working harder than ever. The proud Delta staff didn't understand how the company could be losing money. Workers were increasingly frustrated, and it wasn't long before accusatory fingers were being pointed at the marketing division.

We ended the "meet or beat" campaign and decided to selectively match competitor fares where it made sense. Things stabilized somewhat, but the company was barely back to break even. We had to do better, so we evaluated absolutely everything. We examined the fleet mix (we had too many big planes flying too infrequently), advertising (it was lifeless), and schedules (we had too many planes on the ground for too long during the day). All these problems would be addressed, but it would take time, and, at best, solving them would provide only incremental improvements. We needed a big hit, and we needed it fast.

The financial status of the company was reviewed in periodic status meetings, which were often painful because the news was not good. At these meetings, however, I began to notice what I called "the yield/load factor seesaw." Airline performance is measured by two basic metrics: yield is the amount of money the airline gets per passenger mile, and load factor is the percentage of seats filled by paying passengers. In the status meetings, it would be reported that "yields are up, but load factor is down." This triggered the pricing department to match all low fares in the market and the reservations people to increase the number of discount seats made available. A rational response, we thought.

The next month, load factor would be up and yields would be down, but revenues were still flat. The pricing people were instructed to resist matching the deepest discounts, and the reservations staff was told to limit the number of available discount seats. This also made sense—it did no good to fly full airplanes at fares so low we couldn't make money. But then, the next month, the situation reversed again. We rode the yield/load factor seesaw up and down again and again, but the company simply wasn't moving forward. Revenues remained lackluster. The situation was clearly becoming critical, and concern intensified by the week.

The yield/load factor seesaw intrigued and puzzled me. I was convinced that an answer to our problems was somewhere in this equation. Investigating further, I discovered fifty people working feverishly at computer terminals on the fourth floor of the reservations building. This group was called "Reservations Control." They were charged with interpreting directions from the status meetings to either add or take out discount seats.

I spent quite a bit of time observing this group. These "inventory controllers" sat at their computer terminals all day long and studied future flights. They adjusted the number of discount seats available on future flights up or down, depending on the results from the latest status meeting. They were told to add or take out discount seats, but nobody told them how many. These controllers had a great deal of discretion on how they allocated discount seats on any particular flight, since each market and each flight were so different.

The inventory controllers were a bright group of people with a lot of experience in the markets they worked. Most of them were former reservations agents—changing discount seat inventories required typing cryptic computer entries into a secure, password-protected reservations system, and this ability was taught primarily in the reservations department.

The elements that affect revenue—price and inventory availability—were separated at Delta, as they were at most airlines at the time. The pricing department decided the number of fares and the fare levels for a particular city pair (e.g., New York–Boston). The inventory people independently decided the number of seats that would be made available at those fares for each individual flight. In effect, the inventory people were determining which fares would actually be brought to market. Theoretically, the pricing department could set the fares it wanted, but if the inventory people didn't assign many seats to these fares, the pricing action was virtually irrelevant.

It hit me almost immediately that nobody understood the impact these inventory adjustments had on revenue. The number of discount fares and the number of seats offered at each discount varied by day of week, time of day, and season. A flight might have only a handful of discount seats, or it might have practically all discount seats. The number of discount seats was determined solely by the judgment of the inventory controller. Several factors—such as the number of competitors on the route, who the competition was, and the strength of passenger demand on a particular flight—were considered, but the actual inventory allocation was based on the gut feel of the controller.

It occurred to me that the real pricing war was being fought here in the trenches. The fifty people pecking away at their reservations terminals all day were actually the soldiers in what was really a secret pricing war. The controllers thought they were just shifting seats around to meet demand—just controlling inventory. But actually they were determining how much revenue each flight would bring in.

The problem crystallized for me when I watched the inventory controller work Flight 727 on the Washington, D.C. to Atlanta route. I had flown this flight many times when I was practicing law. It was a "briefcase special." Because of the nature of business in Washington, the briefcase crowd flying back and forth between Atlanta and Washington usually books its seats on short notice and is not very sensitive to price. Flight 727 was a perfectly timed 5:30 P.M. departure from Washington National Airport. On weekdays, it was virtually 100% full of briefcase traffic. But because the briefcase crowd habitually books only a few days before flying, Flight 727 showed a lot of unsold seats when the inventory controller reviewed it two weeks before a departure date.

When the order came down from the status meeting to increase discount seats, the inventory controller would look at Flight 727 and similar flights two weeks before departure. Panicking over the number of unsold seats, he would assign more seats to discount categories. Ten days later, the flight filled up, much to the controller's relief. What the controller had no way of knowing was how many of Delta's core business customers were turned away because the flight filled up with discount passengers. Some of these people would have been willing to pay any amount of money to get on that specific flight. In other words, the controller didn't have a clue about the revenue impact of his decisions.

When I asked the inventory controllers how they determined the number of seats to offer at each fare level, they told me that they just used their own judgment and experience. They had no forecast of future demand for each flight. True, they could look at the passenger numbers from previous similar flights, but without revenue figures showing the impact of their decisions, the historical data was essentially useless.

At the time, Delta had 550,000 flight departures annually, so each controller was personally responsible for discount seat allocations for 11,000 future departures. Because of this tremendous work volume, it was impossible to look at every flight individually, so simplifying assumptions were made. For example, New York–Dallas was considered a business market, so the number of discount seats would generally be restricted. Micromarket differences by day of week (the weekends generally had few business travelers) and time of day (Sunday night had plenty of businesspeople) could not be closely analyzed.

The New York–Florida route, on the other hand, was a highly competitive "leisure market." These flights were loaded with plenty of discount seats. But no special consideration was given to the price-insensitive business commuters who spent the week in New York working and the weekends in Florida relaxing. They would fly to Florida on Friday afternoon and back to New York on Monday morning almost on a weekly basis during the winter season. The inventory controllers tried to account for some of these differences at the micromarket level. However, the number of flights and the diversity in the markets were just too great for them to account for everything.

I realized that we were downgrading thousands of seats from full fare to discount unnecessarily. In doing some quick, back-of-the-envelope calculations, I figured that if Delta was discounting just one seat unnecessarily on every flight, that translated into *$52 million in lost annual revenue.*

The problem was complex. The fifteen hundred daily flights Delta operated at the time added up to 86 million seats for the controllers to manage on an annual basis. Meanwhile, the market was getting more chaotic every day. Competitors were entering and exiting markets at a dizzying pace. Fares were changing so rapidly that their average life was only ten days. Each flight had different characteristics based on season of the year, economic factors in the cities served, departure time, and day of week. Managing these factors would require a dynamic review and reassessment of discount and inventory decisions.

Passengers also had a wide range of individual characteristics. Some cared more about the departure time than about the fare. Others wanted the cheapest fares; to get them, they would shift times, days of week, or even destinations. Competitors would do anything to gain an advantage, including providing frequent-flier goodies to gain the loyalty of business passengers or using rock-bottom fares to steal market share. This was war.

In the reservations building, the fifty inventory controllers were not prepared for war. They fought in the trenches but didn't understand the nature of the war and its objective. No one had told them that their job was to maximize revenue. They had no training, no sophisticated weaponry, and no real intelligence about the battlefield. Management, on the other hand, was operating strictly on the big-picture level. Execu-

tives had very little information about the micromarket side of
the operation. The most management could do under these
conditions was to watch the skies and turn on the siren when
missiles from the competition headed our way.

By now, this yield/load factor seesaw problem was driving
me crazy. I talked to everyone involved in seat inventory processes—including inventory controllers, and people in pricing,
reservations, field sales, and airport operations—gathering all
the information I could. In the end, I was convinced that an
astronomical amount of money was slipping through the company's fingers. Looking at just a minuscule sample of Delta's
annual flights revealed a lot. Some flights that had been loaded
with discount seats sold out well in advance of the departure.
But on these flights, Delta would also turn away significant
last-minute, full-fare traffic. This added up to a lot of lost
revenue. Also, on numerous occasions we had severely limited
discount fares and ended up sending flights out with empty
seats that could have been filled with discount passengers.
Again, a major revenue opportunity missed.

I estimated that Delta was leaving as much as $200 million
a year on the table, just from misallocating discount seat
availability on its flights. This number was so mind-boggling,
I didn't dare tell anyone. No one would have believed it!

GOING AFTER THE MONEY

I knew we had to get the money being left on the table, and
we had to get it fast. But doing so meant a major change in
thinking. It meant becoming revenue driven and developing
the ability to make dynamic decisions at the micromarket
level. At this level, inventory decisions could not be made on
broad, mass-market assumptions because they would not ap-

ply to a significant number of individual flights. We needed to consider the individual characteristics of every single flight, every single day. Decision making had to get more sophisticated—new computer systems would be needed. Gut feel and seat-of-the-pants decisions wouldn't cut it anymore.

I figured that to get started we needed an investment of about $2 million in people and systems. A figure of $200 million annually in increased revenue was too much to promise, so I cut the figure in half, then halved it again. But this number—$50 million—still sounded a little too high, so I made my case to Delta's management based on a likely return of $40 million. This was more believable and easily supported the required investment.

The potential impact of this new activity was exciting. It gave me the opportunity to test a two-pronged approach: first, to use computers to accumulate and analyze huge amounts of passenger booking data, and second, to organize and educate the inventory controllers, transforming them into a new breed of supply/demand specialists who were the nucleus of our RM team. One of the first questions we had to answer was whether we should give the decision-making function to managers or arm the soldiers in the trenches. Management decided to arm the soldiers.

The task of this RM team was to break through the uncertainty paralyzing many airlines. This meant establishing a new way of viewing our business, a new way of organizing information, and a new way of controlling the destiny of the company. We would have to forecast customer demand preferences and the price/convenience trade-offs they were willing to make. We had to turn the uncertainty of the constantly changing market into probability and be able to act on that probability for every single flight, every single day.

Our first automation efforts were crude by today's standards, but it was a good start. Because of the urgency imposed by the red ink, we initially concentrated on simple things that would provide the biggest return. A huge database was assembled to store all historical bookings, as well as "snapshots" of the current bookings on future flights. We established standard booking profiles against which the computer compared all future flights every night. The next day, the computer would tell us which flights were booking more slowly than expected and alert the controller to make more discount seats available. It would also indicate flights that were expected to fill up with higher-fare traffic and recommend removing discount seats. Although it was not the rocket science Delta uses today, the computer could scan all this future flight information daily to identify where the revenue opportunity was. Thanks to the new technology, it was the first time we could look at every individual flight every day, a year into the future. It would have taken hordes of controllers to do that manually.

Changing the mind-set of the inventory controllers was another critical element. Generating the additional $40 million depended on their cumulative ability to make the right decisions on every flight they controlled. This wasn't easy. Many times, it involved changing the value of only one or two seats on a two-hundred-seat aircraft. It was critical that the inventory controllers understand that these were bottom-line issues and that they become responsible for the impact of their decisions. They had to understand basic supply/demand economics because they were, in effect, mining revenue at the margin. We developed an intensive education program to refocus the controllers on this new way of thinking. They could not be mere seat allocators anymore. Instead, they had to be revenue controllers, responsible for knowing their markets from every standpoint. They had to behave more like commodity brokers than airline employees.

Within three months, we dismantled the yield/load factor seesaw. The new revenue controllers had only one fundamental charge: "Get the most money from the most passengers on every one of your future flights." They had to understand the dynamics of their flights. They had to predict the value of each seat based upon the constantly changing elements in the marketplace. They had to anticipate when the flights would need more discounts in order to sell out. More important, they had to know when to turn away discount seekers and save seats for full-fare passengers who might book a month later. They had to learn that sometimes a bird in the hand is worth *less* than two in the bush.

Some people just couldn't handle this responsibility. Others were champing at the bit to get at it. We had been chasing yield. We had been chasing load factor. Now we would be chasing revenue. We were going to be *revenue driven!* This involved a major shift in thinking.

Before long, the impact of the revenue controllers was being felt throughout the organization. One day, Delta's comptroller, Julius Gwin, called and demanded to know what we were doing "down there." He had been studying the numbers and couldn't figure out what was happening. He knew something was making the numbers jump, and he thought that we might have something to do with it. We did. Our little group of fifty-six people, in a company that had about fifty thousand employees at the time, was making the numbers jump like they had never jumped before.

As it turned out, even my private estimate of the potential return was low. In one year's time, Delta realized an incremental revenue gain of *$300 million* solely from the new seat inventory control process. Not a bad return on an investment of a few million dollars. This $300 million accounted for half the $600 million turnaround Delta reported in fiscal 1984.

The experience at Delta was a revelation for me. We had discovered something extraordinary—the Rosetta stone of revenue generation. The power of this process to maximize revenue was mind-blowing. At the time, I thought that Delta was behind the rest of the industry in using these concepts, but I soon found out that all airlines were only just beginning to tackle the difficult issues associated with discounting.

I also realized that these revenue-generation techniques had tremendous potential for application to all kinds of businesses. Every business discounts its prices at some point in time. That's a fact of life in today's business world. No company gets full price for all its products all the time. But questions about discounting are complicated. How low do you go? How many do you sell at the low price? How much product do you save for customers who may be willing to pay more? In other words, how do you make sure that you're selling the right product to the right customer at the right time for the right price?

Looking at every single transaction to find the answers to these questions is a monumental task for any company, no matter what size. That's why marketing managers typically approach these questions through a series of assumptions and deductions based on their experience and observation. They use whatever information is available and broadly apply their conclusions to vast segments of the market. They believe that it is impossible to look at every individual transaction in every micromarket in excruciating detail, so it is necessary to make simplifying assumptions. But this kind of "gut feel" decision making can be dangerous, as the experience of the major players in the airline business have shown. Now, a new way of addressing the difficult strategic questions faced by every company makes it clear that marketing can and will become less of an art and more of a science. With an intense focus on revenue and rapidly evolving computer technology, a whole new way of generating profits is suddenly at hand.

This is powerful stuff—so powerful that I decided to start the first company devoted entirely to the art and science of Revenue Management. The judgeship would have to wait.

CHAPTER
3

THE CORE CONCEPTS OF
REVENUE MANAGEMENT

Revenue Management has proven to be a devastatingly effective competitive device.
—DR. ALFRED KAHN, ECONOMIST; FORMER
SENIOR STAFF MEMBER, PRESIDENT'S COUNCIL OF
ECONOMIC ADVISORS; FORMER CHAIRMAN, CIVIL
AERONAUTICS BOARD AND NEW YORK PUBLIC
SERVICE COMMISSION

THE ORIGIN OF REVENUE MANAGEMENT THINKING

OVER THE PAST FIFTEEN years, Revenue Management has evolved from being a rudimentary economic practice to the incredibly sophisticated tool now used in major corporations. But the basics of RM thinking have been known for a long time. In fact, the essential concept has been in use for as long as commerce itself.

Consider, for instance, a transaction conducted by a woman working in the world's oldest profession, somewhere around 6000 B.C. It's easy to imagine the exchange with her customer: a price and duration was established, with the service provider trying to maximize the return from her most valuable asset—her time. She probably had a limited number of customers, and forecasting the evening's business would have been relatively straightforward.

As newer professions emerged, the marketplace dynamic was pretty much the same. In fact, from an economist's point of view, not much has changed in the last eight thousand years with respect to generating revenue for any service or product. The ability to get the desired revenue from the market is subject to basically the same variables that existed in ancient times. The strength of customer demand, the quality of the products, the availability of alternative products and services, the time of day, the day of the week, and the season of the year—all are critical factors in determining price.

Few significant advances in these revenue maximizing concepts were made until the Scottish economist Adam Smith published *Wealth of Nations* in 1776. Smith wrote of the invisible hand that guides consumers and suppliers, each acting with enlightened self-interest, to make efficient use of scarce resources. In Smith's market economy, the participants in the marketplace seek information to make individual decisions that promote only their own interests. The producer seeks to maximize profits. The consumer wants to minimize costs. Neither realizes that together they are promoting the interests of society by employing resources for their most productive use.

More than one hundred fifty years after Adam Smith, Austrian economist F. A. Hayek laid the theoretical groundwork for modern Revenue Management in "The Uses of Knowledge in a Society" (*American Economic Review* 35, September 1945, pp. 519–530). Hayek explained how profit-maximizing companies can take advantage of temporary opportunities in the marketplace created by what he called "special circumstances of the fleeting moment," which may not be known or recognized by others. In simple terms, this means having market information your competitor does not have and using it to your advantage.

This is essentially what we were doing at Delta when we first became serious about focusing on revenue. It's also what Bob Crandall, CEO of American Airlines, and others were exploring when they developed what they called "yield management."

As many of this country's most forward-looking executives now understand, capturing these fleeting opportunities should be a basic business practice. Some of the opportunities are obvious, but most are not. Many involve looking into the future and accurately predicting what will happen. Sometimes, a decision to forego near-term opportunities results in greater long-term gain. Frequently, this involves turning away immediate business to save products or services for later, more valuable customers. It's an opportunistic mind-set, and it's becoming more important to businesses every day.

THE RM ATTITUDE

Revenue Management is a new way of approaching the age-old problem of supply/demand management. How do you best match your productive capabilities to the demands of the market? Economists would define RM as a means of allocative efficiency that maximizes economic wealth through dynamically forecasting the self-seeking activities of each individual consumer. I prefer a simpler explanation:

REVENUE MANAGEMENT DEFINED
_____

Revenue Management is the application of disciplined tactics that predict consumer behavior at the micromarket level and optimize product availability and price to maximize revenue growth.

In even simpler terms, Revenue Management ensures that companies will sell the right product to the right customer at the right time for the right price.

On a practical level, RM is a micromanagement tool that enables companies to turn mountains of disparate marketing data into tactical intelligence, allowing them to take advantage of the fleeting opportunities of the marketplace. While this often involves setting up large-scale computer systems to analyze and predict customer behavior, RM is not a computer system. It is an integrated set of business processes that brings together people and systems with the goal of understanding the market, anticipating customer behavior, and responding quickly to exploit opportunities that present themselves.

A successful application of the RM approach can involve astonishingly sophisticated technologies. But because attitude and mind-set are so essential, RM can also work at a surprisingly simple level. In fact, as the following three examples show, RM is a strategy that can be used successfully at no-tech, low-tech, and high-tech levels.

CAROL'S BARBERSHOP— A NO-TECH APPROACH TO RM

Carol Meinke used to operate a one-chair barbershop in the rural town where I have lived for many years. She was somewhat of an institution in the local community, being both a talented hairstylist and a great lady. I liked to have Carol cut my hair but dreaded visiting her shop. Since I frequently travel during the week, I could go to Carol's only on Saturdays—but Saturdays were especially busy at Carol's small shop, as retirees convened there to review Friday night's high school football game and whole families waited patiently for their turn in the single barber chair. For people like me on a tight schedule, Saturday mornings at Carol's were frustrating. It was sometimes a two-hour wait to get my hair cut. I tried to talk Carol into accepting appointments so that people could schedule specific times to get a haircut without waiting, but she did not want to change her fundamental approach and risk alienating her customers.

One day, I spoke to Carol about this Saturday problem and explained the basic principles of Revenue Management to her. Together, we summarized her situation:

- The shop was overcrowded on Saturdays, but Tuesdays were very slow.
- Some of the Saturday customers, like myself, could come only on Saturday; others were retirees and schoolchildren, who could get their hair cut any day of the week.
- Her rent and utilities costs were increasing, but many of her customers would balk at an across-the-board price increase.
- Carol was turning away a significant number of customers on Saturday. This was lost business opportunity.
- Carol had considered adding another chair and part-time barber to the shop, but she couldn't justify this cost.

Over the course of a few months, I tried to convince Carol to experiment with Revenue Management techniques. I urged her to raise her prices on Saturdays and discount them on Tuesdays. My belief was that there were those of us who were willing to pay a premium for the convenience of a Saturday haircut and that others would gladly move to a weekday to save a few dollars. To put it in RM terms, this would recognize the price/convenience trade-offs that I assumed existed in Carol's micromarkets.

At first, Carol was reluctant to change the prices because she thought that her customers would not accept paying different prices on different days of the week for what she believed was essentially the same service. But one Saturday, as Carol was cutting my hair, a man stuck his head in the doorway and, seeing all the chairs in the waiting room filled, turned around and left. I asked Carol if she knew him. "No," she said.

"He's not one of your regulars?"

"No," she said again.

"Well," I told her, "he never will be. You lost a customer not just for today, but for life. He'll find another barber and you'll never see him again." Right then and there, she decided to give Revenue Management a try.

Here's what Carol did: she raised prices on Saturdays by 20% and lowered prices on Tuesdays by 20%. The retirees and mothers with school-age kids were delighted to move to Tuesdays for a lower price. This filled the slack in Carol's Tuesday schedule and enabled her to serve Saturday customers who were willing to pay extra for convenient Saturday service. She was able to retain many of the people who used to leave frustrated on Saturday without getting their hair cut. Furthermore, customers who continued to get their hair cut on Saturdays (like me) benefited from a waiting time that was reduced to less than thirty minutes. Most important, at the end of the first year of this arrangement, Carol was astonished to find that she had increased the overall revenue of her shop by almost 20%!

THE WASHINGTON OPERA—
A LOW-TECH APPROACH TO RM

Located at the Kennedy Center for the Performing Arts in the nation's capital, the Washington Opera is one of the top professional opera companies in the United States. The 1993–1994 season, however, did not meet the company's financial expectations. The combination of an orchestra strike and bad winter weather resulted in an unanticipated deficit, which the company had to make up in the next season.

New money had to be found to make up the deficit. The standard remedy for revenue shortfalls in performing arts organizations is to raise ticket prices across the board 5% or more. But Jimmy Legarreta, the ticket services manager of the opera company, resisted doing this. "We realized that we couldn't raise our prices every year any more," he recalls. "There comes a point when our patrons are going to say, 'Enough is enough.' " Legarreta had never heard of Revenue Management, but he realized that if the opera raised prices across the board, it risked losing midweek patrons, and the result could be less revenue, not more.

With the blessing of the company's director, Patricia Mossel, and armed with information from the company's automated ticketing system, Legarreta set out to find a new way to increase revenue. This was the situation:

- The budget for the 1994–1995 season was about $12 million.
- Sixty percent of the revenue had to come from ticket sales. Ticket sales also affected allied revenue streams (e.g., ticket-holder contributions, membership fees for various support groups, lecture fees, functions, and other activities).
- The company produced seven operas per season. Four were presented in the twenty-two-hundred-seat opera house and three were performed in the smaller, eleven-hundred-seat Eisenhower Theatre. Because of scheduling limitations at the Kennedy Center, no additional performances could be scheduled.
- Tickets were historically sold at three pricing levels: orchestra, first tier, and second tier.
- Friday and Saturday night performances were routinely sold out. In fact, the company had to turn down requests for seats on those nights. A significant number of seats to midweek performances were not sold, and the company often "dressed the house" with employees to fill in the audience on slow nights. Many midweek ticket holders also sought to convert their tickets to weekend performances, which increased administrative costs.

Legarreta's strategy involved two major parts. First, determine the "value" of each seat, and then, price each seat according to what the customer would be willing to pay. "We knew that all the seats in the house did not deliver the same experience," Legarreta says. "You cannot say that every seat in the theater has the same value. It's simply not true. The last row on the extreme side of the orchestra level is not worth the same value as the tenth row center." Legarreta and his staff literally sat in every seat in the theater and evaluated each location according to the acoustics and the visibility of the electronic unit over the stage that provides simultaneous English translations.

After Legarreta analyzed the results of his research, he installed nine pricing levels, each targeted to different micromarkets. Legarreta increased the ticket prices for seats worth considerably more than previously charged (some seats went up by 50%) and lowered the prices on 660 seats (including a number of orchestra seats). Before, tickets were sold at one of three prices—$47, $63, and $85. Tickets now ranged from $29 to $150, making the opera accessible to just about everyone. Legarreta also addressed the midweek/weekend demand differences with pricing differentials that would encourage some patrons to buy tickets for midweek performances, thereby freeing seats on Fridays and Saturdays to accommodate previously turned-away demand for those nights.

Without realizing it, Jimmy Legarreta was, in effect, employing classic Revenue Management techniques. By adopting this RM attitude, the Washington Opera increased its revenue by about 9% for the 1994–1995 season, almost twice what would have been the optimal result of a 5% across-the-board price increase. The plan produced a couple of other impressive firsts: the company sold every prime orchestra seat and more than 90% of the tickets for the entire season (sixty-four performances) by September, two months before the season opened; and the renewal rate for season subscribers was an unprecedented 94%.

AUSTRIAN AIRLINES—
A HIGH-TECH APPROACH TO RM

Austrian Airlines has been one of the most consistently profitable airlines in Europe. Even in 1991, when the Gulf War sent
most airline profits down the tubes, Austrian Airlines turned
in its twenty-first consecutive year of profits, illustrating its
ability to operate successfully in an industry that is highly
cyclical. But new challenges are on the horizon for Austrian. A
form of deregulation in Europe is vastly changing the competitive landscape for several European industries.

Executives at Austrian Airlines saw this coming a decade
ago; they recognized that the European airline industry would
eventually move to a much more competitive environment.
They set out to develop a plan not only to survive but to win
in the deregulated environment. Studying the impact of airline
deregulation in the United States, they determined that the
winners were the revenue-driven airlines. So far, so good—but
meanwhile, the airline's situation was very challenging:

- Austrian lacked a large network of domestic routes, so
  it had to find new ways to continue to compete with
  aggressive and larger European, U.S., and Asian international carriers.
- The company operated approximately thirty aircraft of
  varying sizes.
- Extensive reservations data was available from Austrian's reservations system, which was operated with
  Swissair.
- The airline knew that there was additional revenue opportunity from higher-fare business travelers but did
  not know how much.

THE SEVEN CORE CONCEPTS OF REVENUE MANAGEMENT

1. Focus on price rather than costs when balancing supply and demand.
2. Replace cost-based pricing with market-based pricing.
3. Sell to segmented micromarkets, not to mass markets.
4. Save your products for your most valuable customers.
5. Make decisions based on knowledge, not supposition.
6. Exploit each product's value cycle.
7. Continually reevaluate your revenue opportunities.

CORE CONCEPT #1: FOCUS ON PRICE RATHER THAN COSTS WHEN BALANCING SUPPLY AND DEMAND.

Supply/demand imbalances plague virtually every company. It is almost impossible to achieve a perfect balance between the amount of product you offer and the market's desire for your product when and where you have it available. Even if you are successful in striking that balance, it won't last long in today's amoeba market. The tendency for many companies encountering supply/demand imbalances is to remedy them by the use of capital assets. Airlines are a prime example. If airline traffic increases, airlines are quick to order new aircraft. If traffic falls off, cancellations and deferral of aircraft deliveries are the results. The airlines virtually never get it timed right, and the industry is in a state of almost continuous oversupply. In addition to ordering more aircraft, airlines are quick to shift planes from one market to another in an effort to chase passengers, even passengers who will fly only on deeply discounted fares.

Hotel companies ride much the same cycle. They acquire properties during prosperity and divest in a downturn. They staff up for peak periods and lay off staff afterwards. Too often, they focus on managing costs, not exploiting revenue opportunities.

These tendencies are not limited to the travel industry. Manufacturers expand production capabilities when business is looking up, then they close plants when profit pressure increases. For smaller or shorter-term supply/demand imbalances, companies of all kinds still try to remedy the imbalances by redeploying capital, adding staff in peaks, and discharging employees in the off-peaks. These are viewed as rational responses to swings in the marketplace, but they often prove to be costly reactions to short-term situations. And they increase internal entropy. Such tactics are not always the best way to address supply/demand imbalances. Sometimes, using price as the lever to balance supply and demand can be much easier and a lot more profitable.

One major freight company in the United States has demonstrated the inefficiencies of using capital rather than price to correct temporary supply/demand imbalances in the market. Known for relentless cost control, the company thoroughly evaluates every operational movement and improves it to the nth degree. Activity-based costing determines such things as how many steps the delivery man should take from the truck to the door and in what order the keys should go on the drivers' keyrings.

The revenue side of the equation, however, has not received the same degree of scrutiny. Much of the company's business is with large, bulk shippers, who dispatch millions of small packages annually. Typically, the sales department negotiates one- or two-year contracts with these large-volume shippers, and it is not unusual for final contract negotiations to include a hefty 15%–25% across-the-board discount.

Many of these shippers are catalog merchants who have tremendous seasonal peaks, moving 30% or more of their annual business in the five or six weeks just before Christmas. In preparing for negotiations with these shippers, the freight company calculates the average cost of shipping the antici- pated volume of packages from the catalog companies' ware- houses to the typical destinations. The discount rate is applied to every package shipped during the contract period, regard- less of the season of the year and the demand on the resources of the freight company.

During the Christmas period, the freight company doesn't have the capacity to handle the increased volume of packages. It routinely arranges for short-term capital to lease aircraft and to acquire ground transportation and sorting facilities during this period to meet its delivery obligations. The com- pany goes to extraordinary lengths and great expense to add the staff, equipment, and facilities to handle the peak demand, but it doesn't pass these incremental costs on to the shippers. The catalog company shippers pay the freight company the same low, discounted rate during this period.

Some of these catalog companies, however, recognize the opportunity to charge more. A number of them charge their customers a surcharge for holiday and rush shipments. These shippers become, in effect, arbitrageurs, capitalizing on the willingness of their customers to pay more during peak peri- ods. The freight company not only misses out on incremental revenue, it has to bear the additional cost of capital to meet the requirement of the peak season.

If the freight company became revenue driven, it would spot these opportunities to charge more during the peak period around Christmas. Slightly increasing its shipping rates during Christmas would do two things: encourage price-sensitive traffic that did not need to move during the Christmas season to be shipped outside the peak window, and help fund the additional cost of providing the extra service required during the peak.

Opportunities for incremental revenue increases are everywhere. Often, personal observation—not technology or extensive databases—is all that's required. But to see these opportunities, you must have a market-centric focus. When Carol Meinke was faced with high demand for haircuts on Saturday, she considered hiring help on the weekend to accommodate the extra demand. To offset the slow period on Tuesday, she could have closed half the day and not lost too much business. These would have been typical cost-focused approaches to leveling demand peaks and valleys. Instead, she chose to apply innovative pricing to attract price-sensitive customers to Tuesday and charge more for time-sensitive customers on her peak day. Applying this simple concept allowed her to generate more revenues on both Tuesdays and Saturdays. The result was that her weekly revenues were up sharply, without any incremental cost.

The hospitality industry provides an example of another successful, relatively low-tech approach to using price rather than capital to balance supply and demand. Hotels that serve primarily business travelers are very busy during the week and empty on weekends. The traditional approach to this problem had been to significantly cut staff to reduce costs on the weekends. Of course, much of the fixed overhead continued. Marriott Hotels pioneered innovative weekend "products," which offer low rates designed to attract customers from the local market to the hotel. Using programs such as "Two for Breakfast" (a 50% room rate discount), Marriott has generated incremental revenue by filling rooms that otherwise would have been empty.

Since airlines have such high capital costs (a typical airplane can cost $100 million), they are becoming adept at high-tech approaches to using price to balance supply and demand. Using sophisticated mathematical modeling, they can forecast passenger demand on a real-time, micromarket basis, shifting discount seats from high-demand flights to low-demand flights. Delta, for example, now forecasts passenger demand on nine hundred thousand future flights each day to reallocate discount seats as market conditions change. Although Delta and virtually every other airline still use capacity adjustments to account for demand swings, such adjustments are made only if discounting does not sufficiently address the demand imbalance.

Whatever your business, adjusting prices, not costs, should be your first line of attack when trying to get the supply/demand balance right.

Tactic for Market Domination: Use Price Balancing

Conventional Wisdom:	In times of high demand for your product, increase productive capacity. If demand falls, reduce capacity.
Entropic Event:	Demand fluctuations grow in frequency and intensity.
RM Tactic:	Address short-term fluctuations first with price, then with capacity.

CORE CONCEPT #2: REPLACE COST-BASED PRICING WITH MARKET-BASED PRICING.

The natural inclination of all companies is to price their products based on the cost to produce, sell, and deliver them. The theory is that if we can recover our costs plus a certain percentage from each of our customers, we can guarantee our margins. This is the ultimate dream for all businesses—guaranteed margins.

But consumers, quite frankly, don't give a damn about our costs. Customers put a certain value on goods and services based on their own unique needs and desires. A consumer's perception of value will be colored by a myriad of factors: availability of alternatives from competitors, amount of disposable income, and the urgency or need (real or perceived) for the product. If the price we place on the product exceeds that value, customers don't buy. It's that simple.

Most companies are so caught up in their own issues of costs and are so corporate-centric in their perception that they haven't taken the time to understand the perspective of the consumer. What a consumer cares about is value, and each consumer defines value in his or her own terms.

Hotels are a case in point. Historically, hotels set rates according to the cost of the construction of a room; for example, they would charge $1 for every $1,000 of construction cost per room. A hotel with one hundred rooms that cost $7 million to build would therefore establish a daily room rate of $70. Later, rates in the hotel industry were set in terms of the position of the hotel in the market relative to physical assets and amenities, not market demand. Now, the RM approach is revolutionizing pricing.

A good example is the Radisson Park Terrace, an elegant,

intimate, 200-room European-style hotel in Washington, D.C. For years, the Radisson Park Terrace refused to discount its rooms, even though it had an average occupancy rate (percentage of rooms filled) of about 50%. In the view of the hotel management, the rooms were worth the high rate it consistently charged, since the Park Terrace had the appeal of a five-star hotel. It was obvious, however, that potential guests didn't always place the same high value on the rooms at this hotel. Some nights, the hotel was full. On many nights, however, it was virtually empty.

Basing room rates on the concept of market demand was an alien thought for the Radisson Park Terrace, even though the hotel was losing $2 million a year. When new management took over in 1989, it implemented a pricing program internally called Value Management. This strategy was a classic implementation of Revenue Management's market-based pricing techniques. When demand was high, prices stayed high. When demand dropped, discounts were offered to fill rooms that might otherwise go empty. Soon after the new pricing approach was begun, occupancy rose from the 50% range to nearly 80%. Thanks to Value Management, now the Radisson Park Terrace routinely reports profits of over $500,000 a year.

Price and price setting have traditionally been issues of great concern for companies, and for good reason. A 3% increase in price, without loss of volume, can increase the bottom-line profit by 20% or more! Some companies have scores of analysts studying the pricing problem. They look at production costs, carrying costs, distribution costs, and margin requirements, as well as the way the company is positioned against competitors. They evaluate and reevaluate all these factors to come up with a price they think will stick.

But who really determines the price at which your products

will sell? Not you! The old rules of cost-plus pricing no longer apply. The power in pricing has clearly swung to the consumer. The consumer decides the price and the conditions he or she will accept. And the definition of what is acceptable will vary tremendously for any product, depending on the consumer's circumstances at any particular point in time.

Consumer behavior, of course, is notoriously difficult to predict. The factors that drive the buying decision and the price the consumer is willing to pay are not necessarily linked to demographics or psychographics. The same individual— say, a professional/managerial white female between the ages of twenty-five and forty-nine—can exhibit multiple behaviors when buying the same commodity. Take the case of Ms. Smith, a lawyer. For years, Ms. Smith has been a regular customer at a popular restaurant in Atlanta that is renowned for its traditional Southern cooking. She often takes clients there for dinner during the work week, and on at least one Saturday a month Ms. Smith and her family of five go there for lunch. Last month, Ms. Smith even attended a local bar association dinner at the same restaurant.

The dinner menu at this restaurant is priced significantly higher than the lunch menu, even though Ms. Smith's favorite food items are exactly the same on both menus. Her client dinners are business related and can be expensed, so she is not concerned about the cost of dining at the restaurant during peak-priced weekday evenings. However, she does not take her family there for dinner but instead considers the lower-priced lunch menu on the weekend affordable for a family meal. For her bar association dinner, she paid the reduced fixed price negotiated by the bar association. Ms. Smith is the same person with the same demographic and psychographic profiles and buys the same meal each time she visits the restaurant. But, depending on the circumstances of time and place, her consumption behavior varies.

How many companies know what the view of the consumer toward price will be today, tomorrow, and every day into the future? In other words, *how do you price for uncertainty?* Some companies, like Hertz Rent-a-Car, have employed a "see what sticks" pricing strategy. For decades, the car rental companies made their money on such things as favorable tax credits, sales of collision damage insurance to renters, and sales of used rental cars. Now, as competition intensifies, car rental companies are faced with having to make money actually renting cars. To make matters worse, the airport car rental business is highly price sensitive, consumers have a wide range of choice, and fleet acquisition costs have risen dramatically (for Hertz alone, up 60% in 1993–1994 and another 30% in 1995).

Alarmed at the cost increases and downward pressure on profits, Hertz announced across-the-board price increases in March 1993, again in September 1993, again in March 1994, and again in September 1994. Feeling the same price pressures as Hertz, competitors followed suit on each attempt. Guess what? The consumer didn't care about the cost pressures of Hertz and its kin, and they let the car rental companies know it. Bookings dropped off substantially after each price increase. Consumers forced price roll-backs, and deeper-discount promotions were launched to get renters to return.

Still looking for higher revenues, Hertz tried another price-raising tactic. In 1995, it brought back mileage fees. Remember them? That's when you pay a daily rate plus a certain amount, like 25 cents, for every mile driven after a free-mile allotment. But consumers didn't like it, and two months later, mileage fees were dropped.

Just because you place a price on your product doesn't

mean that you establish the price. The market (i.e., the consumer) establishes the price, and your job is to find the market's acceptable price point. You can try to enhance the perceived value by improving the product or positioning it as better, faster, or sexier. But in the end, consumers will let you know the price they are willing to pay at any point in time. They will either buy or not buy at the price you place on the product. Intimate knowledge of the market (and micromarkets) helps you determine the price points that are acceptable to nonconformist consumers and that will give you a suitable return. If they don't buy at the price point that gives you an acceptable rate of return, you need to take another course of action.

The "great cat food war" is a case in point. In the mid-1980s, in response to competition from Quaker, Nestle, Grand Metropolitan, and others, Heinz cut the price of its 9-Lives Cat Food 24%—from $6.77 to $5.25 a case. More price cuts followed as competition heated up. At Heinz, soon the discounted prices weren't covering its increasing production costs. Someone in the company decided that it was time to revert to the traditional "cost-plus" pricing formula, and in 1991 Heinz hiked its prices on 9-Lives. But Heinz's customers resisted the price hike, and Heinz's market share dropped from 23% to 15%. It was a wake-up call about who was in charge of cat food pricing, and it wasn't Heinz. If Heinz wanted to stay in the cat food business, it had to figure out what the customer was willing to pay for 9-Lives, change its manufacturing process to meet that target price, and still make money. They had to change from cost-based pricing to price-based costing. The company did just that, and in 1994 Heinz's cat food revenue jumped from $41 million to $55 million. Market share went up to 25% that same year.

Using market-based pricing doesn't always mean that you

have to cut prices. Sometimes, the market will allow prices in excess of the cost-plus formula. This is why companies must understand consumer behavior at the micromarket level.

TACTIC FOR MARKET DOMINATION:
USE MARKET-BASED PRICING
_____

Conventional Wisdom: Set prices to cover costs and provide an acceptable profit margin.

Entropic Event: Nonconformist consumers determine the price they are willing to pay; market provides numerous choices.

RM Tactic: Forget cost-based pricing. Set prices consumers will accept in a price-flexible environment; reduce costs, if necessary, to meet margin requirements.

CORE CONCEPT #3: SELL TO SEGMENTED MICROMARKETS, NOT MASS MARKETS.

In the long run, overall costs must be brought to a level that can support the market price of the products a company offers. In an aggressively competitive market, however, certain opportunities can provide companies with a revenue advantage despite an apparent cost disadvantage. The objective in business today is to deliver what the consumer wants faster, better, and cheaper than anyone else. But this faster-better-cheaper mantra will help only if companies understand that not all customers want the same thing. The mass market is, for all practical purposes, dead. In its place, we now have millions of individual market segments.

Market segmentation is the key to market-based pricing and revenue maximization. Segmentation is most often defined in terms of demographics (age, sex, income, education, occupation, etc.) and psychographics (attitudes, life-style, personality, etc.). These have been useful concepts for purposes of product creation and target marketing. But for purposes of market-based pricing, what we really want to know is: *What is the customer willing to pay?*

An individual consumer's willingness to pay for a product may reflect his or her demographic and psychographic profile, but the actual buying decision will be dictated more by the individual's current circumstances. These will vary tremendously over time. So the question becomes: *What is THIS customer willing to pay for THIS product at THIS point in time?* The answer depends on the universe of variables in the market, which can be determined by observation.

In the amoeba market, there's an enormously diverse market for any product. Every individual has a different reason for wanting the product, different plans for using it, and a different idea of its value. Revenue Management strives to determine the value of the product to a very narrow micromarket at a specific moment in time. The objective of RM is to chart customer behavior at the margin to determine the most revenue that can be obtained from that micromarket at that moment in time.

Some people may not value the product or service very highly. You're not going to get much revenue from these customers; in fact, you may not want to sell to them at all, unless the sale disposes of excess inventory, in which case you'll discount it and get the price down to the customers' perceived value for that specific use at that moment in time. To other customers, however, the perceived value of your product may be high, which means the actual value of your product also changes based on the consumer demand at the moment of sale. In other words, you can't set the value of your product. You can only set the price, and the price you set must coincide with each customer segment's perception of value.

Every product exhibits some degree of price elasticity in various market segments. This is not a revelation, it's basic economics. The lower the price, the more goods you will sell; the higher the price, the fewer goods sold. The mistake that most companies make is trying to arrive at the appropriate average price for the average consumer. There is no average consumer. Therefore, you should not set an average price.

PRICING ECONOMICS 101

The following charts demonstrate why average pricing makes little sense.

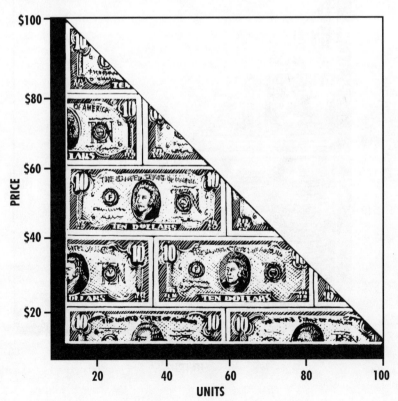

For any product, there is a downward-sloping demand curve that describes how many units of the product will be sold at any given price. In this simplified example, if the price of the product is placed at $99, only one unit will be sold. As the price drops, more units are sold, until the price gets to $1; then, ninety-nine units are sold. (See chart on page 73.)

According to conventional wisdom, a profit-maximizing firm would charge $50 and sell fifty units. This would generate $2,500 in revenue. Under this scenario, forty-nine people are willing to pay more than $50, and one consumer would even be willing to pay $99. The amount that people are will-

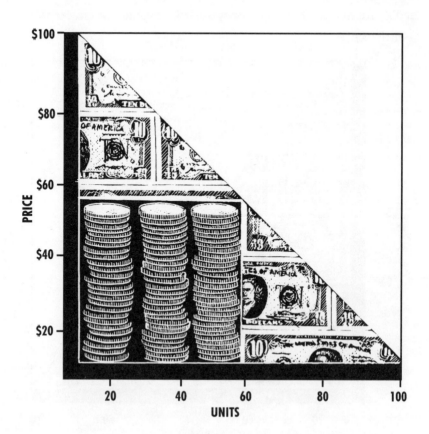

ing to pay in excess of what they were charged is called "consumer surplus." That is missed revenue opportunity for the company. Note that there are forty-nine people willing to pay less than $50, but they are refused—another missed revenue opportunity. (See chart on page 74.)

If the company were able to segment its customers by willingness to pay, and charged four different prices rather than only one, it could generate significantly more revenue from its existing capacity, without making any other changes to the product. Under this demand scenario, the company could sell twenty units at $80, twenty at $60, twenty at $40, and twenty at $20. This would result in revenues of $4,000, a 60% in-

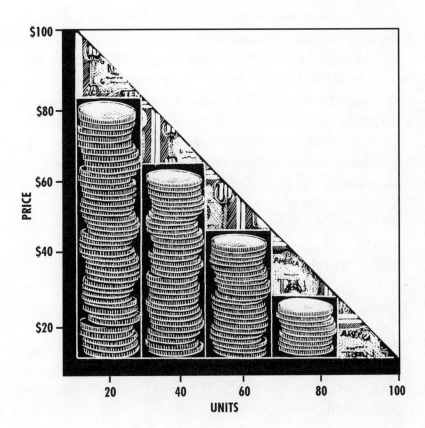

crease. Theoretically, if every customer was sold the item at his or her individual price point, the company could achieve $4,950 in revenue. (See chart on page 75.)

Segmenting markets by willingness to pay is not a new concept. It has been done in some fashion by virtually all companies for many years. It is a rational way for producers of goods to increase the revenue they get from a diverse marketplace. The objective is, and should be, to segregate consumers who are willing to pay full price for the product from those who value the product less. But for most companies, the effort to segment markets is primitive when viewed in the context of sophisticated Revenue Management techniques.

One low-tech approach to market segmentation is through discount coupon promotions. For example, breakfast cereal makers offer coupons that represent significant savings. The coupons are designed to encourage the purchase of the cereal by those who would not ordinarily buy it, without disturbing the shelf price for the consumers who are willing to pay more. These coupons may represent discounts of 50% or greater. Another approach involves "midnight sales," which appeal to price-sensitive furniture and appliance buyers while separating them from consumers who value convenience of time more than price. Another example is the discounted weekend rates offered by car rental firms. All these efforts are simple attempts to exploit the diversity of the marketplace.

These common strategies use known and apparent market differentials to set price differentials. But how are the differentiating factors and discount levels set? Do they efficiently address the increasingly fractionalized marketplace? Do they account for subtle differences with respect to the amoebic micromarkets? Do they instantly respond to the changing behavior of the nonconformist consumer?

RM moves beyond basic market segmentation and responds to the realities of today's exploding micromarkets. In this arena, the difference between getting it right and getting it *nearly* right in terms of the resulting revenue can be staggering. For the furniture and appliance industry alone, for example, a 1% price error could cost the industry $120 million annually.

TACTIC FOR MARKET DOMINATION: USE SEGMENT PRICING

Conventional Wisdom:	Price should be set to sell the greatest number of units at the highest possible price in the mass market.
Entropic Event:	Consumer individualism shatters the mass market.
RM Tactic:	Different segments demand different prices. To maximize revenue and stay competitive, prices must vary to meet the price sensitivity of each market segment.

CORE CONCEPT #4: SAVE YOUR PRODUCTS FOR YOUR MOST VALUABLE CUSTOMERS.

One of the most costly concepts in business is that of "first come, first served." Virtually all companies have this policy in some aspect of their business. "First come, first served" is relevant only when there is a shortage of product available. Otherwise, everyone who comes is served. Companies know they must have some way to decide who gets access to goods in high demand, and to the unsophisticated eye, "first come, first served" seems as good as any other method to them.

"First come, first served" is perceived as fair for both companies and consumers. Aren't the ones who get their hands on a product first the most deserving? Aren't they obviously the customers who value the product the most? Many think so. It makes no difference whether we are talking about tickets to a rock concert, the initial production of the latest model car, or a table at a restaurant. In restaurants, for example, the first to arrive is the first seated. Even if the restaurant takes reservations, the person who is first to make the reservation gets priority for the tables. (Hospital emergency rooms are, thank goodness, an exception to this rule. They usually try to assess the need of the individual for critical care in deciding who gets served first.)

The problem for businesses is that it is precisely those times when they have a shortage of product that they also have the greatest opportunity to maximize revenues. But all customers are not created equal. A popular restaurant, for example, could conceivably fill its tables with nondrinking dieters (low revenue) and turn away heavy-drinking gourmands (high revenue) simply because a crowd of low-drinking dieters happened to arrive first. In very peak periods, such as New Year's Eve, the restaurant may impose a cover charge or require a minimum order per person—a crude form of Revenue Management. But on most nights, it is a victim of chance. What the restaurant has unwittingly done—and in fact what rock concerts and sports teams and virtually all other businesses who see long lines for their product do—is segment its market by willingness to come early and stand in line, not by willingness to pay. This is not revenue optimizing!

I've seen some very costly applications of the "first come, first served" policy in a number of industries. For example, one rental car firm would routinely sell its last car for a one-day Wednesday rental (the peak day for business rentals). Sometimes, the next phone call would be a request for a seven-day, weekly rental that would have to be denied because the company was out of cars. Worse, the cars it rented on Wednesday would sometimes sit idle all week so they would be available for the Wednesday reservations.

In many market segments, the people who are least likely to pay the highest price are those who will seek to purchase it first. This is especially true in industries where consumers are spending discretionary dollars. They will trade off their time for your money. If you have excess inventory, this may not be a bad deal. But if you have a shortage, even if a very temporary one, you should find a way to predict which segments are willing to pay the most and save those products for them.

Sea-Land, the international shipping company, uses what it calls "reefer teams" to ensure that it achieves as much revenue as possible from its products, which in this case are transported cargo containers, or reefers. In Sea-Land's case, the challenge is not to save productive assets for its most valuable use on a *fixed* network, such as scheduled airline and rail services, but to maximize revenue from its assets within a *flexible* network. Sea-Land has a number of options on how to get the shipment to its destination.

Problems arise when full reefers are sent to a location where there is no return cargo available to fill them for shipment to another destination. To address this problem, the company established the cross-functional reefer teams to focus on the critical objective of maximizing revenue. These teams use computer modeling to identify spikes of unmet demand, to prioritize incoming business (i.e., deciding what business should be rejected to enhance the overall revenue result), to identify the margins for determining equipment allocation, and to arrive at the optimum fleet size for greatest flexibility and revenue generation. The company is determined to match its most valuable products with its most valuable customers.

TACTIC FOR MARKET DOMINATION: FAVOR THE MOST VALUABLE CUSTOMERS

Conventional Wisdom:	Sell products and services on a "first-come, first-served" basis.
Entropic Event:	Traditional business practices don't satisfy investor demands for aggressive revenue growth.
RM Tactic:	Understand demand at the micromarket level as accurately as possible, and save products for the most valuable customers to achieve optimum revenue.

CORE CONCEPT #5: MAKE DECISIONS BASED ON KNOWLEDGE, NOT SUPPOSITION.

Many companies have collected data about customer transactions for many years, and many corporations are now using sophisticated information management techniques to interpret this data for decision-making purposes. Collecting information, after all, is not enough; to be useful, information has to be processed and converted to knowledge. In some quarters, this movement from "information" to "knowledge" is beginning to take place.

Whether a company is a family-owned convenience store, a sports team, or a $20 billion corporation with the latest high-powered computers, knowledge-based decision making can be critical to success. Deciding what products to offer at what price should not be left to hunch and supposition in today's fast-changing marketplace. Data must be collected, interpreted, used to predict future consumer demand, and reviewed to ensure the best possible decisions.

The power of the systems that store, manipulate, and analyze massive amounts of data can be staggering. The typical Revenue Management database for a major airline can exceed 300 gigabytes of data, which is equivalent to a stack of paper 6,350 meters tall (the Matterhorn is a mere 4,477 meters high). One person working forty hours a week and spending only five seconds per page would need over forty-three years to scan this amount of data. Revenue Management systems glean the relevant pieces of data from huge databases like this every single working day. These gigantic RM databases capture and store every customer transaction and house facts about consumer behavior and market conditions in infinitesimal detail.

Not every company, however, needs to be so ambitious. Data sampling can be done in a variety of ways. A sandwich shop owner probably does it subconsciously based upon random observations. He may notice that the chicken salad doesn't seem to be moving as well since he raised his price, and he may be tempted to lower the price. He needs accurate information about sandwich unit sales and revenues. He may resist rescinding the price increase if he notices that his chicken salad revenues are higher despite lower unit sales.

What's most important is to adopt a Revenue Management program of appropriate size and scope. Whatever this is, the first task in implementing a Revenue Management solution is to gather as much data as possible about consumer behavior and the market you're in. By itself, this data won't do much. It must be disaggregated, reaggregated, sorted, filtered, and analyzed. Next, the application of sophisticated mathematical forecasting techniques could allow you to predict future customer activity.

Companies that access and analyze information about their transactions, their consumers, and their markets are astonished at the difference it makes. A clear picture of actual consumer behavior minimizes biases and conjecture in decision making. Product and pricing options must be considered with a much clearer eye.

Many companies are starting to wrestle with the same issues addressed by Revenue Management, even though they may not use actual RM tactics. Compaq Computers is clearly one such company. In 1994, Michael Parides, director of business operations in the desktop computer division of Compaq, searched for a way to manage the lightning-fast changes taking place in the personal computer business. A misstep in pricing, product features, timing, demand assessment, and distribution can kill a PC manufacturer. The window of opportunity for a new PC product is so volatile that it can sometimes be measured in mere days.

To make sense of the chaos and uncertainty of the PC market, Parides created a computer program that simulates demand elasticity, price changes for components, demand/price fluctuations, inventory trends, and competitive actions. These simulations were meant to assist Compaq in assessing the

probable outcomes of specific marketing and product decisions before these decisions are made. Reportedly, Compaq
used Parides's simulation modeling software later in 1994,
when the company made the decision not to rush machines
based on the Pentium chip to the market. The simulation
model predicted that corporate customers would wait until
early 1995 to buy Pentium-based products, which meant that
Compaq would have time to sell its substantial inventory of
machines equipped with the earlier-generation 486 chip.
Fourth-quarter 1994 earnings rewarded this decision to the
tune of a 61% *improvement* over the previous year's quarter.

But creating the simulation software and having it accepted
by the company as a decision tool was not an easy proposition. It involved changing the corporate culture, gathering and
examining an unprecedented amount of data, and challenging
established marketing and sales practices and decision-making
philosophies. The decision to delay bringing the Pentium PCs
to market, which was made after months of testing the simulation model's conclusion, was a clear rejection of the argument made by the sales force that the Pentium introduction
should be accelerated for competitive reasons. In effect, management made a counterintuitive decision and embraced the
simulation model's findings.

The RM tool that enables you to make decisions on knowledge, not supposition, is forecasting. It is essential to predict
consumer behavior if you are going to exploit opportunities in
the marketplace. Better forecasts mean better business decisions, and better business decisions mean greater profit. A true
forecast should be a prediction of what will happen, independent of what you think will happen or what you want to
happen. Significant gains have been made in the application of
statistical data analysis to generate more-accurate forecasts of
future market behavior. Such forecasts provide a detached,

unemotional view of the market. Good forecasts reduce the uncertainty about the future, and very good forecasts convert this uncertainty into probability.

Many executives believe their markets are so chaotic and things are happening so fast that it is not possible to forecast what will happen. This is a lame excuse. Every manager has to make some predictions about his or her markets to make rational decisions. These may be based on either intuition or personal observation, but they must reflect some kind of market assessment.

What often appears to be random and chaotic can have discernible patterns if you know how to look at the data properly. Take your average traffic jam. The particular cars sitting in traffic around us on any given day are randomly distributed. The traffic jam will comprise different people in different vehicles from one day to the next. But you can be sure that there will be traffic delays at particular times on particular roads on particular days.

Humans, for the most part, are lousy forecasters, subject to both intentional and unintentional biases. They may forecast a higher sales volume than is appropriate because they hope sales will be high. They will give inappropriate weight to information that is more easily accessible (e.g., an offhand remark by a colleague) than information that may be more important but more difficult to obtain. Increasingly, however, the most significant human limitation is our inability to digest the huge and growing amounts of information about our customers and our markets especially as they become more fragmented. But thanks to computers, this limitation can be largely overcome, making accurate forecasts possible.

No matter how powerful the technology, of course, there will always be some error in a forecast, because consumer behavior will never be 100% predictable. There will always be the need for humans to understand and interpret the statistical analysis done by computers to reduce forecast errors. The objective of good forecasting is to use both human intuition and analytical tools—a combination of art and science—to achieve the best possible forecasts that enable the best possible decisions.

TACTIC FOR MARKET DOMINATION: FORECAST AT THE MICROMARKET LEVEL

Conventional Wisdom:	General assumptions can be made about future consumer behavior based on intuition and personal observation.
Entropic Event:	Nonconformist consumers are continually fragmenting the market and changing buying behavior.
RM Tactic:	Forecast demand at the micromarket level to gain knowledge of subtle changes in consumer behavior patterns.

CORE CONCEPT #6: EXPLOIT EACH PRODUCT'S VALUE CYCLE.

Once you have a good forecast of your customer's behavior, how do you make the best of it? How do you maximize the value of your product in the micromarkets over time? In other words, how do you exploit each product's value cycle? Here's where optimization comes in—the RM tool that answers the question about what actions will produce the best results under the current forecast of consumer activity.

During my initial work in the area of optimization a decade ago, Revenue Management development was still in its information stage. At that time, my colleagues at Aeronomics and I would collect and store huge amounts of data, and our principal task was to make sense of the data by product and market segment. The sorted and filtered data then went to market analysts, who would make better decisions based upon better information. This process produced significant revenue gains.

But two factors concerned me: the huge number of decisions that had to be made on a daily basis in the thousands of submarkets and the fact that the decisions were highly complex. In the airline, hotel, and car rental businesses, for example, the most valuable persons are the last to book, and seats, rooms, and cars have to be saved for these last-minute, high-price customers. How could this be determined? This question proved very difficult to answer. Over time, I realized that it was critical to remove some of the human biases from the decision making while still allowing human judgment to be part of the process.

One day, about a year after I started my Revenue Management company, en route to a client I met Dr. Ren Curry. Coincidentally, we were both going to see the same airline client. I was providing consulting services on Revenue Management, and Ren was consulting on aircraft performance.

Ren had been a research scientist at NASA—a genuine, card-carrying rocket scientist who had developed guidance systems for space vehicles, as well as some very efficient mathematical models to optimize the reentry flight path of the space shuttle. I was struck by the similarity of his thinking about optimal flight paths and my ideas about the need for optimal decision-making tools in Revenue Management. Up to this point, airline staffers had been given better information and even some rudimentary forecasts, but airlines were still relying on human judgment to make the actual decisions about how many discount seats to sell on any given flight. Was there such a thing as an optimal revenue curve that could make airlines millions? Ren and I concluded that maybe there was.

Later, I asked Ren for his assistance on a major RM project. Working together, we discovered that there were numerous applications of rocket science optimization techniques to marketing issues. These applications could vastly increase the speed of decision making and in most cases lead to better decisions than those made by humans alone. The difference these applications could make in optimizing a product's value cycle to increase revenue generation was clearly enormous.

From a purely mathematical viewpoint, the forecasting and optimization problems posed by RM are far more complex than those involved in a space shot. The laws of physics don't change from here to the moon or from one day to the next, but the nonconformist consumers in an amoeba marketplace change constantly. No computer model can account for all the variances. But then, no human can handle the volume and complexity of the decisions. It follows that Revenue Management systems (computer models) work best when used by market specialists (humans) to produce solutions far better than either would derive alone. Still, the analogies between rocket optimization and revenue optimization are so striking that I have found it useful to explain the concepts of revenue optimization in terms of rocket launches.

Because of the current limitations that rocket engine technology imposes on scientists, it is impossible to get a typical payload into orbit with just one booster rocket. Multiple stages are required to progressively move the payload to higher altitudes at higher velocities. Each stage builds on the momentum of the previous stage until the speed and altitude needed to reach orbit is achieved—about 17,500 miles per hour at 125 miles altitude (27,350 km/hr at 201 km altitude). Escaping the earth's gravitational pull altogether is even harder. The escape velocity is about 25,000 miles per hour (40,200 km/hr).

Fuel accounts for about 95% of the weight of the rocket, and, of course, the burning fuel provides the necessary acceleration to get the spacecraft into orbit. A delicate balance is essential. If too much fuel is loaded, the rocket will be too heavy to be propelled into orbit; with not enough fuel, it will fall short. Because no extra fuel can be carried, it is vital that the firing of each rocket stage happen precisely at the optimal moment.

If the second stage is fired too soon, the unburned fuel in the first stage has been wasted. The first stage will not have propelled the vehicle to the altitude and velocity necessary, and orbit will not be achieved. If the second stage is fired too late, momentum from the first stage is lost. Again, orbit won't be achieved. The fuel in the second stage must be spent to regain the momentum rather than take the ship higher. The same is true with subsequent stages. There is a specific, optimal point at which to fire each stage in the course of a launch. This point must be calculated by mathematical formula. The success of the mission depends on the proper calculation and execution of that firing sequence.

Revenue optimization operates under the very same principles. Instead of fuel, think of revenue. We are going up the revenue curve of a product's value cycle, and we want to achieve maximum revenue velocity and altitude. In other words, we want to get *as much money as possible, as soon as possible*. Unlike a space shot, however, we aren't satisfied with merely getting into orbit (making a profit), we want to

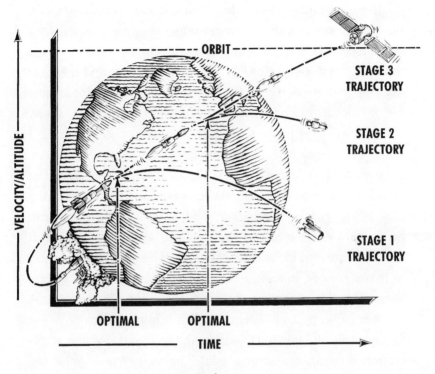

Rocketry

maximize the revenue we get from our product. Each stage of our revenue rocket is an identifiable submarket from which we want to attain the greatest possible revenue velocity and altitude. We must be assured that we will obtain the maximum revenue desired from each.

Let's look at the entertainment business to see how the concept of revenue optimization can be applied to the value cycle of movies. When a movie is made, the producers expect revenue from a variety of sources, mainly theater screenings and home video. The primary, most valuable market is the theatergoers—these customers will pay dearly to see the movie as it is released. Less valuable are customers who will wait for the video. The producers need to get the most they can out of the theater segment before the video is released. If they release the video too soon, they miss out on some of the revenue they could have received from theatergoers. If the video is released too late, interest in the movie will have declined, and the revenue opportunity is reduced. There is an optimal point in time for the movie studio to release the video. The question is how to determine that point. Currently, it's not rocket science. It's based on judgment and experience.

Now, look at the issue in terms of revenue rocketry. The launch of the movie into the theaters is analogous to the firing of the first stage of the rocket. The revenue achievement can be thought of in terms of velocity and altitude—how much money is flowing in, and at what rate. This will be a function of many factors, including the subject of the movie, the stars headlined, the quality of the production, the promotion, the number of screens on which the film shows, and so on.

Assuming the movie is successful, the initial revenue acceleration is great, but after a while, no matter how good the movie is, the revenue stream from the movie decreases as that stage of the value cycle plays out. Before it slows to zero (indicating a complete lack of interest in it), the video must be launched. The optimal point for releasing the video can be determined by forecasting (and reforecasting) the trajectories of the various stages (micromarkets) and calculating the timing and price point combinations that would result in the optimal revenue given the current and forecasted velocity and altitude.

This concept can apply to virtually any product whose total market can be divided into submarkets that place different values on the product. The product itself doesn't have to be physically different; you only need to be able to make some distinction between one offering of it and another to price and control it differentially. For example, when would the movie producer make the movie available to cable and network television? These are separate market segments with their own revenue trajectories and therefore are separate stages subject to optimization.

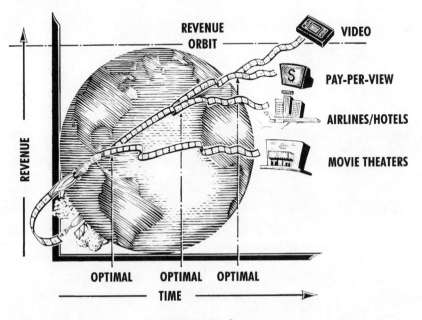

Revenue Rocketry

Not every company needs to employ the complex algorithms used in space shots in their everyday business problems, but you should attempt to see how the revenue rocket analogy applies to you. This requires three steps: (1) breaking your business into logical stages (submarkets), (2) projecting a revenue trajectory for each stage, and (3) determining the optimal time to launch the subsequent stage. Take, for example, a clothing store. For each new line of clothes, the store owner might have three stages in the pricing process: a rack price for the market segment that is fashion conscious, a 20% discount offer for the less fashion conscious, and a 50%-off discount bin for the budget-conscious segment. The expected revenue trajectories could be initially set for each and monitored over time. The timing for moving the merchandise through the different stages should be established with the objective of achieving the optimal revenue at each stage.

TACTIC FOR MARKET DOMINATION: MAXIMIZE REVENUE THROUGH OPTIMAL TIMING

Conventional Wisdom:	Decisions on product availability and pricing are made on experience, gut feel, tradition, or rule of thumb.
Entropic Event:	Rapidly changing market conditions defy conventional approaches.
RM Tactic:	Generate maximum revenue by understanding the value cycle and optimally timing the availability and price of the product to each micromarket segment.

My company has conducted tests that have pitted human "experts" against a computer programmed to calculate optimal revenue from product value cycles. The computer consistently won in every instance because it could precisely locate the optimal point on each revenue curve. In fact, the computer produced revenue increases of 5%–10%. Humans are just not able to accurately calculate the mathematical optimum on a regular basis.

There will always be an art to running a profitable business. But as the marketplace becomes ever more complex, managers must learn the science of business too—and the concepts at the heart of rocket science can teach us a lot about how to optimize revenue.

CORE CONCEPT #7: CONTINUALLY REEVALUATE YOUR REVENUE OPPORTUNITIES.

The frenzied pace of the amoeba market does not allow the luxury of carefully prepared plans that are then implemented faithfully by the minions. Wars are not won by generals operating in remote strategy rooms far from the heat of battle. Similarly, market wars are not won by strategists in corner offices—they are won in the trenches by the foot soldiers battling with your competitors every day. Many of these wars will be sudden and unexpected; competitors will use surprise to try to gain advantage, perhaps by offering a special discount to a key customer. And you are in constant danger of losing customers to stealth competitors you are not even aware of.

I often advocate the creation of massive databases that have the ability to evaluate every transaction. For large companies, the competitive wars of the future will be won by analyzing micromarkets and taking advantage of the opportunities in each narrow market at a particular point in a product's value cycle. These opportunities necessarily will be fleeting, and success or failure will depend on your ability to capitalize on them by responding instantly.

The case of the Canadian Broadcasting Corporation (CBC) will illustrate core concept #7. As a public broadcasting company, CBC is charged by the Canadian government to meet the educational and cultural needs of the public. However, it must also compete with commercial broadcasters for advertising dollars. Because of its unique situation, CBC decided to explore Revenue Management techniques to find a way to maximize its revenues.

CBC manages one national and four regional television networks, plus seventeen individual market TV stations. Seventy salespeople across Canada sell approximately 2,040,000 advertising spots annually. CBC's RM system processes 170,000 commercial spots monthly and provides forecasts up to ten months into the future. This data is interpreted and analyzed in a timely manner, enabling CBC to react quickly to market changes and to update pricing as soon as a revenue opportunity arises. With RM, CBC uncovered new revenue-generating opportunities, including installing weekly pricing capabilities that fluctuate with demand and identifying advertisers willing to pay a premium for specified inventory. Different pricing and inventory decisions can be made for each week up to fifty-two weeks in the future and continually reevaluated—a revolutionary concept in the television broadcasting industry.

Before RM, CBC always had lower yields than its competitors. In 1988 it started to use demand to price its products and saw immediate revenue improvements. After the introduction of the RM decision support system in 1992, the yield for CBC's inventory exceeded that of its competitors, even though CBC's audience share is smaller than that of its competitors. Normally, the underdog doesn't sell at the higher unit price; it's usually the other way around, with the leader charging the premium.

Continually reevaluating your revenue opportunities does not necessarily require huge databases and powerful computers; no-tech RM tactics can always be applied by heads-up entrepreneurs. Jim Compton, a revenue manager for Continental Airlines, relates a story about how his daughter used a dynamic application of market knowledge and demand-based pricing to exploit a revenue opportunity. "The subdivision I live in had a neighborhood garage sale a couple of weeks ago," he told me recently. "Kristin, my seven-year-old daughter, decided to set up a lemonade stand for this event, and it was interesting to watch her in this first entrepreneurial experience. She started out charging 5 cents a glass at 8:00 A.M., when there weren't many people and she was not getting many customers. By noon, however, she noticed that there was more traffic and, as the temperature started to rise, people were making a beeline for the stand because they were hot and thirsty. She immediately bumped the price to a quarter and sold a lot of lemonade at that price all through the afternoon."

This girl understands the fundamentals of Revenue Management! Kristin could have been satisfied with merely selling more lemonade at 5 cents. But her awareness of customer behavior patterns (people get thirsty on a hot afternoon) led her to respond dynamically to the marketplace by changing the price of her product after reevaluating her revenue opportunities. In true RM fashion, she took advantage of a fleeting moment in the marketplace.

Advanced Revenue Management is merely an extension of these principles. In its most sophisticated form, RM takes huge databases of consumer information and gives companies knowledge of probable consumer behavior and thus wisdom to make an optimal response. An RM manager's job is to establish the mission, provide the tools, coordinate the activity, and ensure that objectives are met. However, the day-to-day decision making—where the battles will be won or lost—must be at the micromarket level. Critical speed is replacing critical mass in capturing marketing opportunities. Shortening the time frame for decision making is paramount. In this environment, decisions cannot be sent up the ladder to a higher commander because it takes too long for the decision to come back down. Giving the person on the front line far greater access to far more relevant, timely information enables him or her to continually reevaluate the state of the amoeba market.

This is not to say that the decisions must be actually made in the field. Today's advanced information technology can provide the same data at several locations at the same time. Headquarters can look at the same data the field location looks at. This enables a company to have the best of both worlds—decentralized decision making at a central site.

TACTIC FOR MARKET DOMINATION: ARM THE SOLDIERS FIGHTING THE MICROMARKET WARS

Conventional Wisdom:	Information in the hands of a top manager ensures that the best decisions will be made for the company.
Entropic Event:	Breakdown of the mass market occurs, and the need for fast response at the micromarket level increases.
RM Tactic:	Give decision-support tools to the workers in the trenches to make dynamic decisions at the micromarket level.

Despite the intensive involvement of high-powered computational capabilities, the role of people will not be not diminished in companies adopting Revenue Management. In fact, people will be more important than ever. Computers will handle much of the gathering, collecting, and disseminating of the data. Additionally, computers will make the routine decisions and provide assistance on complex problems. But the role of a revenue controller will be critical, although it will change dramatically.

Currently, computer systems play a decision-support role in a company, providing access to data and sorting and filtering relevant information for a controller to analyze. As mentioned earlier, people find it difficult to distinguish bias from fact and have trouble dealing with huge amounts of data. The strength of computers offsets these weaknesses beautifully. Where people have desires or fears that might bias the interpretation of information, computers are purely rational. Where people can be overwhelmed with information (a study by Bell Labs showed that humans have trouble effectively handling more than seven numbers at once), computers can crunch millions of bits of information with relative ease.

Computers are wonderful machines, but they are limited. They are extremely literal. They will do exactly what you tell them, even if it's wrong or illogical. Computers can solve the same problem over and over thousands of times without tiring, but they are incapable of exercising independent judgment. Humans, on the other hand, can assess a completely new situation and rely on experience and judgment to react accordingly. Computer systems that can "learn" have been developed, but they generally don't adapt to changing circumstances nearly as well as humans could.

Companies often have to react quickly to major changes in the marketplace that could never have been foreseen under normal forecasting procedures. Computers are poor at responding to unforeseen events; they are severely limited by the data in their database. Although they can handle enormous amounts of data, computers don't have access to every fact that might be relevant. How can a computer react to rumors in the market that might affect the value cycle of your product? While "game theory" is becoming popular in assessing potential competitive strategies, it will be a long time, if ever, before computers will really be able to anticipate the movements or responses of your competitors. Such knowledge comes from years of experience in the market.

Human beings have the initiative and boldness that can capture the imagination of consumers and put fear into the hearts of competitors at the same time. In companies adopting RM tactics, computers will do what they can do best—analyze millions of bits of disparate data at a micromarket level and make recommendations or decisions. If properly designed, they will identify the exceptions that require human judgment and intervention. The computer will do the grunt work. Its human operator will make sure that the computer is assessing the market properly and will fine-tune and correct for things the machine may not account for. This will free a company's staff person to do what he or she does best—be innovative and creative in responding rapidly to the dynamic demands of an increasingly chaotic marketplace.

With people and computers working hand in hand, the payback from the practice of Revenue Management is tremendous, not only in incremental revenue but in knowledge of the market at a greater level of detail than ever before achieved. And though the RM technology can be complex, the core concepts of Revenue Management are simple. Every company that wants to dominate its markets in the future must understand and apply them.

4

CASE STUDY: THE ATTACK
OF THE LASER FARES

*If we don't invent an answer to this, we're history. We're
going to be dead meat.*
—DONALD BURR, CHAIRMAN AND CEO,
PEOPLEEXPRESS AIRLINES

WAR

THEY CALL HIM "FANG"
and "Darth Vader," a fierce Goliath who "faces his accusers
with guns ablazing," engaged in a contest that he himself describes as "intensely, vigorously, bitterly, and savagely competitive." His opponents believe his strategies are
"cannibalistic." They believe his mission is to "kill the weak."
They think he "sees himself as the enforcer."

This tough guy who eats nails for breakfast isn't Attila the
Hun, Saddam Hussein, or the Terminator. He's the CEO of a
major U.S. corporation. The comments weren't reported by a
war correspondent but by a writer for *Business Week*. And he
was referring to Robert L. Crandall, chairman of American
Airlines.

War—that's really what it's all about in today's business world. The generals, captains, and lieutenants may wear gray flannel suits and carry black leather briefcases, but they're still fighting a war. Every day, they march off to a new battle over some piece of turf, and the headlines of the *Wall Street Journal* scream about bombs being dropped, predators swooping down on their prey, winners and losers, bloody battles in the boardroom, and wounded companies. In every corner of the marketplace, companies are engaged in frenzied activity to win at all costs. For some, this new kind of cold war is exciting as hell. For others, it *is* hell. But make no mistake about it—it's war all right.

Revenue Management first played a decisive role on the modern corporate battlefield in 1985. In the classic tradition of David and Goliath, an underdog took on a giant—but this time, the giant won.

THE INCREDIBLE SAGA OF PEOPLE EXPRESS

When Donald Burr rang in the New Year of 1985, he was riding the crest of the deregulation wave. His no-frills airline gamble had paid off, and now he was a man who had it all: fame, fortune, and the helm of the fastest-growing company in U.S. history. He was an airline man in the most exciting period of U.S. airline history, and he was enjoying every minute.

Then thirty-eight years old, the founder and chief executive officer of PeopleExpress Airlines had a right to be proud. In the four short years since starting his company, Burr had taken an innovative management and marketing concept and single-handedly revolutionized the airline industry. With his ultra-efficient, no-frills airline, he had tapped into an enormous and virtually ignored market for low-cost air transportation, pulling people out of buses and cars and making them air travel believers. Burr had opened the skies to millions of new air travelers by charging prices 50%–70% less than the major airlines. It was a classic entrepreneurial success story.

The previous two years had been especially exciting for Burr and PeopleExpress. The fleet had doubled. There were spectacular traffic gains every single month. Flights were running an average of 75% full. The stock split two for one. On the same day it was announced, a new route to London sold out for months. The company was fast approaching the billion-dollar mark in revenues. At the close of 1984, Burr had just posted his highest twelve-month profit ever.

Success after success after success—it looked like Donald Burr and PeopleExpress could do no wrong. During a period when incumbent airlines were spilling red ink in record amounts, the upstart PeopleExpress, with an off-the-wall operating style and backpacking clientele, had grown and prospered with costs more than 50% below those of the established airlines, and prices to match. Burr had essentially fulfilled the mission of the Airline Deregulation Act of 1978. He was bringing air transportation to the masses, and he was making money doing it.

Don Burr had set up PeopleExpress Airlines to be a reflection of his work philosophies, which had been formed in his childhood and tempered by his experiences as a financier on Wall Street and an executive at Texas International Airlines. He was determined that PeopleExpress would be different. It would be a company that would bring value to its customers and be a fun place to work for its employees.

They were lucky from the very beginning. With record losses and overcapacity throughout the industry, many relatively new aircraft were sitting on the ground, and the owners were in a selling mood. Burr started his fleet with seventeen fuel-efficient, practically new Boeing 737s, which he bought from Lufthansa German Airlines at the incredible price of $3.7 million each, a tremendous discount off the $17 million showroom price. Removing the galleys and first-class sections, twenty-eight more seats were added to each plane. The planes were flown on a rigorous schedule of ten to eleven hours a day, three or four hours more than the industry average for aircraft utilization. Most airlines at the time employed about 149 people for each airplane in the fleet. At PeopleExpress, the number was a modest 57. Burr squeezed every ounce of productivity he could from both people and planes. Pilots and flight attendants rotated into virtually all ground jobs—in marketing, finance, accounting, and ground operations. Pilots loaded baggage. Flight attendant "customer service managers" manned ticket counters when they weren't onboard. Reservations and baggage checking were farmed out because they were considered to be "blue collar" work. Every employee was required to purchase at least one hundred shares of stock as a condition of employment. The real payoff for employees was not the minuscule salary they earned but the rewards of ownership delivered by growing stock values, dividends, and profit sharing.

The product was transportation, pure and simple. All other services, such as checking bags and offering sandwiches and drinks, were unbundled and charged separately to the passenger. These practices alone shaved at least $18 off the ticket price. There were no ticket counters. Tickets were issued and paid for on the plane. The travel agency distribution system— the dominant ticketing force supported by airline commission payments—was completely bypassed. PeopleExpress dealt directly with the people it served. There was a reservations system, but it was rudimentary, storing only the basic information of name and address, flight and date.

"We decided not to invest in automation," recalled Burr. "American and United had been building their reservations systems for over twenty years. They were investing $100 million a year in their systems at the time. We just didn't have the time to catch up. Even if we had the money and the talent, we just didn't have the time."

The company's executive offices were spartan. Burr's office, which doubled as a conference room, rented for $6 per square foot a year, in contrast to office space in, for example, the PanAm Building in Manhattan, which went for about $50 per square foot at the time. As a result of this frugality and productivity, PeopleExpress could put a seat in the air at virtually one-half the cost of other airlines.

PeopleExpress started off from the "dingy and deserted" North Terminal at Newark Airport, a location that was underutilized on the one hand and in close proximity to the highly populated business center of New York on the other. The potential was unlimited. The initial strategy was to steal passengers from buses, railroads, and cars traveling routes like Newark to Columbus, Ohio, or Norfolk, Virginia, both of which had a lot of ground traffic but very limited air service. Thus, the carrier posed little threat to the existing airlines, although Greyhound Bus Lines felt the impact of PeopleExpress from the beginning.

PeopleExpress fares lived up to their advertising claim, "Flying That Costs Less Than Driving," in a simple-to-understand, two-level fare structure, peak and off-peak. "We began by offering low fares that were 50% to 80% lower than the other carriers' fares," explained Burr. "In an attempt to be totally fair to all passengers, we offered the same price to everybody on the plane. It was simple pricing." Tickets from Newark to West Palm Beach were $89 in peak hours and $69 in off-peak hours. In comparison, a bus or train ticket on the same route was in the neighborhood of $130. Using a 20-

cents-per-mile standard, the same trip by car (about 1,250 miles) cost about $250 just for the transportation alone. Not only was flying PeopleExpress a bargain, travel time on the route was reduced by up to 200%!

At first, the established airlines ignored PeopleExpress. They were not particularly interested in the low-yield market segment. Besides, after forty years of regulated competition, their costs were far too high to match PeopleExpress's low fares. By 1983, however, they were paying attention. By that time, PeopleExpress had forty aircraft in the air and plans to add twenty-four more within the next year. Moreover, the average daily load factor on the PeopleExpress route system was an unbelievable 74.6%, compared with the high-50 percentiles of the other carriers.

Having established itself, and with the overwhelming acceptance of low-fare service, the backpackers' airline was now ready to take on the big guys like United and American. Pricing, expansion, and competitive strategies moved into high gear. Clever advertising ridiculed the complicated restrictions of the other airlines' discount fares. In one TV commercial, an agent at the fictional "BS" airlines tells a customer, "You want the BS airlines super low-price special? Okay. Simply fly one way and pay the price you pay the other way if you fly two ways. Okay? Simply put, each way costs half of either way, both ways, some days. Okay?" The traveling public loved it, and the phones continued to ring at PeopleExpress.

By late 1983, the other airlines were becoming very concerned. "We really threatened the hell out of the Bob Crandalls of this world," Burr remembered. "They saw us taking over everything. The response was tremendous! Every market we went into, we became the number one or number two carrier within a month or two of serving the market. We were arrogant about it too. We stuck our chin out and said,

'We are better than you guys and we're going to take you on.' "

As the other carriers began thinking of ways to counterattack, Don Burr did some rethinking of his own. The company had been inundated by customers, and now demand was outstripping its capacity to respond. The growth escalation had caused major problems in the company's system of operation. The reservations department was overloaded. Customers were frustrated because they couldn't get through to book a seat. They still wanted low fares but were growing weary of all the hassle it took to get them.

Things were fast getting out of hand, and it was time to reexamine some of the PeopleExpress start-up philosophies. The company was now moving into a new arena, with domestic aspirations that confronted the established airlines directly and an eye toward international expansion as well.

UNFORESEEN PROBLEM #1:
THE NO-SHOW NUISANCE

The PeopleExpress reservations system was crude by industry standards. Customers who wanted to reserve a seat beyond the ninety-day limit of the system were out of luck. Reservations didn't matter much anyway, since there were no ticketing time limits required to hold seats. As a result, the no-show rate at PeopleExpress was a lot higher than at the other airlines, and PeopleExpress had no way to accurately forecast customer demand. To compensate for this, PeopleExpress regularly overbooked flights by up to 70%.

Airlines had long used overbooking of flights as a means to

combat the no-show problem. With more sophisticated reservations systems than PeopleExpress, however, most of the other airlines could determine the number of seats that could safely be overbooked on a specific flight by studying customer behavior on previous flights. American Airlines had elevated overbooking to a science, even forecasting the costs associated with overbooking practices. But without the ability to collect historical no-show data on its rudimentary reservations system, PeopleExpress was basically overbooking by gut feel. When more customers showed up than could be accommodated, as was often the case, it was not a pretty sight at the gate.

"Ironically," says Burr, "people began to accuse us of being bait and switchers. They were saying, 'You don't have the product! You advertise it, but nobody can get it!' That was true. We didn't have enough product to sell without a more powerful automation system. If people consider it bait and switch to advertise a low fare and then tell callers that it is only applicable on particular flights, then I suppose they would consider it bait and switch to advertise low fares and then tell callers, that, sorry, we are already booked for the next three months."

UNFORESEEN PROBLEM #2:
THE DISTRIBUTION NETWORK

American's SABRE reservations system was making major inroads at travel agencies, which were issuing greater numbers of tickets than ever before. Not only could people have their tickets in hand before they went to the airport, they could have their seat assignments and boarding cards too. The traveling public wanted PeopleExpress's low fares, but they also wanted to be able to get their tickets from their travel agents and arrive at the airport, ticket in hand. And these demanding consumers let PeopleExpress know it.

"They were calling up their travel agents and saying, 'If you don't get me a ticket on PeopleExpress, I'm never going to do business with you again,'" Burr relates. "The travel agents hated us. They started calling us and writing us letters and talking to the press. It was a terrible PR mess that we hadn't foreseen."

Given these two factors and the impact they were having on the expanded company, Burr made two major decisions: first, to start working with the travel agency distribution system on a commission basis and, second, to build a reservations system that would reflect industry standards and would eventually be installed in travel agent locations.

UNFORESEEN PROBLEM #3: INFORMATION SYSTEMS AND CONTROLS

The decision to work with travel agents came after much heated debate among the officer group. Burr felt that the changes were necessary for PeopleExpress to be a player in the new ballgame. Others fought the change. In the end, Burr hired NCR to put on a big push to develop a new reservations system for PeopleExpress that would eventually enable travel agents to book PeopleExpress seats electronically. "They said they could do it and I bought the idea that they could." The timing was critical for the company, and everyone knew it.

But eighteen months later, to his dismay, Burr discovered that nothing substantive had been done. After much debate, NCR was removed from the job, a situation that resulted in the filing of dueling law suits between the two companies.

Burr was beginning to worry. "Now we were in late 1984 with absolutely nothing! We were making money, but we knew we had no answer to what was staring us in the face. We didn't know how lethal it would be." It had been an incredible year for air travel. Close to four hundred million passengers flew on the scheduled airlines, a 10% increase over 1983. PeopleExpress flew over nine million of them, a 62% increase over 1983. It was now wall-to-wall people at the North Terminal at Newark Airport. The facility was practically bursting at the seams. Finally, after two years of intense negotiation, Burr received Port Authority agreement on renovating Terminal C, a facility that would allow PeopleExpress passengers to breathe again on Friday and Sunday nights. But as it turned out, the airline would never occupy Terminal C.

CRANDALL'S CUTTING-EDGE PERSPECTIVE

Like Donald Burr, Bob Crandall also began 1985 on a high note. After twelve years in various executive positions at the giant American Airlines, he was about to be named chairman and chief executive officer, the crown jewel in a career that had included leadership positions in information technology, finance, and marketing. This unusual combination of experience gave him a perspective unique among the members of the industry's exclusive CEO club.

Like most of the major airlines, American had been badly

buffeted by the winds of deregulation, but it had managed to weather the storm in a fairly stable position, thanks to some innovative thinking coupled with Crandall's obsession for strict business controls. As head of marketing for the company, Crandall had searched out every penny of cost and demanded to know what revenue it had produced for the company. In doing so, he gave marketing a new focus: to maximize the return from American's assets.

Crandall's budget meetings were famous throughout the company. Budgeting was an uncomfortable process for the effusive sales types who populated airline marketing departments in those days and who were not used to being held accountable in this way. Managers facing Crandall's cross-examinations on proposed expenditures compared the experience to running a gauntlet on a bed of hot coals. It was just a matter of time before Crandall's intimidating personality earned him some colorful nicknames.

Working for Crandall is definitely a challenge. All business in the office, Crandall is a quick study and although supportive of ideas that are backed up with facts and figures, he has little tolerance for people who come to meetings unprepared to answer the barrage of questions he will invariably ask. He lets his staff know when he's not pleased, often in hair-curling outbursts. As one associate puts it, "They get nailed to the wall." Another says, "If you do it once, you'll never come unprepared the second time."

In the early 1970s, as the government began to relax controls on pricing and routes in preparation for deregulation, Crandall began thinking about what American would need to dominate the industry under the new scheme of things. Earlier in his career, Crandall had developed expertise in information technology and automated inventory control systems, and now he was convinced that the strategic use of automation systems would be the key to marketplace domination. This was revolutionary thinking in an era when computers were viewed as electronic file cabinets or repetitive-task machines.

As head of marketing, and aware of the growing influence of travel agents on airline ticket sales, Crandall sought to develop SABRE into a more strategic marketing tool. At his urging, American's board of directors agreed to invest $300 million to expand the system into a travel agent distribution system. This move, signaling a new era in the marketing of airline seats, caught the other airlines asleep at the switch. Although competitors rushed to develop and sell computer reservations systems of their own, it was very difficult to overcome the SABRE marketplace advantage. As time went on, SABRE took on a life of its own as a major business center for the company; in fact, in some years, SABRE would make more money for American's parent company than the airline itself.

THE BIRTH OF REVENUE MANAGEMENT

By the mid-1970s, public demand for discount airfares increased dramatically. In response, several charter airlines were formed, and because of a flawed fare-setting formula used by the Civil Aeronautics Board (CAB), they were able to offer much lower fares than scheduled airlines. By the winter of 1976, charter fares as low as $99 were available in the highly traveled New York–Florida market, and the charter airlines lobbied the CAB to offer what was called "public charters," which would enable them to sell seats on what amounted to quasi-scheduled service in direct competition with the scheduled airlines.

The threat of the public charters was a matter of great concern for all major airlines, especially high-cost American. Years later, Bob Crandall, who was senior vice president of marketing for the airline at the time of the charter threat, explained the mood. "This was driving us *crazy*. They were going to fly from New York to California for some amount of money that was a hell of a lot less than we had to charge." American had to find a way to compete, but it couldn't possibly produce seats as cheaply as the charter airlines, or so it initially thought.

Crandall called an emergency brainstorming session to probe how American could lower its costs to be competitive with the charter airlines. Late one night, Crandall and his lieutenants reframed the issue. Someone drew a picture of an aircraft on the blackboard. American's planes were currently flying, on average, only half full. That meant that they were carrying millions of empty seats. It dawned on the strategy staff that American was already producing seats cheaper than the charter operators could ever hope to produce. The empty seats they were already flying between New York and California were being produced at a cost of close to zero!

In actuality, American had a revenue problem, not a cost problem. "If we could figure out a way to sell those empty seats at the prices the charter guys proposed," figured Crandall, "we would make a lot of dough." But there were huge problems to overcome. How could they prevent people who were willing to pay the higher fare from switching to the lower fares? And how could they assure that only the seats that would otherwise fly empty (the surplus capacity) would be sold at the lowest fare level?

American devised a plan to address these problems, taking

advantage of its SABRE capabilities. The plan was called "Super Saver Fares," which were capacity controlled, restricted discount fares. Using the inventory controls available in SABRE, American placed a twenty-one-day advance purchase restriction on the special fares so that they would be available primarily to people who booked well in advance of the flight. Additionally, SABRE allowed American to target the discount fares to only those markets and flights where seats would otherwise fly empty.

The Super Saver fares, launched two years before the U.S. airlines were deregulated, were highly successful, and the other scheduled airlines soon followed with similar strategies. Ironically, the public charter threat, American's initial reason for starting the Super Saver program, never really got off the ground. Bob Crandall had effectively defused it.

In formulating a response to the threat from lower-cost competitors, Bob Crandall recognized two significant factors. First, *the cost of each unit he produced was not the same.* Crandall's average costs may have been much higher than those of his competitors, but, because of the volume of seats he produced, the incremental cost of unsold seats was virtually nil. Second, *the market value of his seats varied from passenger to passenger.* There was a significant number of passengers who were not willing to pay an amount that was high enough to cover Crandall's average seat cost. But it would have been suicide to lower the price to *all* his passengers to attract the discount seekers, since there were many other passengers who were willing to pay more than the average price. Thus, Crandall had to segment his passengers in a new way.

Crandall wanted to give these new micromarketing strategies a name. He considered the word *revenue,* but it had already been appropriated by the finance department. He then turned to *yield*, the term airlines used to describe revenue per passenger mile, and he called the strategy "Yield Management." This was the beginning of modern-day Revenue Management.

Although the initial Super Saver fares were very successful, Crandall was not entirely satisfied that they were getting the maximum amount of revenue from each flight. "As time went on," Crandall remembers, "it occurred to us that we had to do a more careful job of managing the number of seats we made available in discount categories."

"We started out with basic allocations," says Barbara Amster, who supervised the project. "Then, of course, you get to the fact that every flight behaves differently by day of the week." Obviously, the Monday morning flight from Dallas to New York would have a different passenger mix than the Tuesday afternoon flight to St. Thomas. Yet it was not uncommon for both flights to have the exact same percentage of seats allocated to discount fares.

By studying the behavioral characteristics of each flight, each day of the week, Amster realized that every flight had to be viewed differently in terms of how many discount seats should be allocated. If a flight was primarily a business flight, then the number of discount seats should be lowered. If it was a flight to a leisure destination, or a weekend flight, the greatest number of potential customers would be discretionary spenders who would be drawn by discount fares.

But to do this kind of study for American's huge route system would require workers looking at mountains of data. They not only had to determine how many seats to offer on each flight each day for up to eight different fares, they had to be able to make changes on short notice if unexpected demand developed, especially at the higher fare levels or if a competitor suddenly came at them with a new discount fare.

The initial systems that American developed for this task were limited, and the company soon decided to start working on the next-generation approach. The plan was to take the overbooking and other models that had been developed and assemble them into a new system that would be called Dinamo (Dynamic Inventory Allocation and Maintenance Optimizer). The essential task was to find a way to accurately forecast passenger demand at different fares, save seats for late-booking high-fare passengers, and allocate the leftover seats to a myriad of fares, some of which would have to be purchased weeks in advance. It sounded simple, but it was a massive problem, and it was not going to be solved overnight. In fact, American spent years of designing, prototyping, and testing.

By the early 1980s, the combination of a mild recession and dramatic capacity increases created a raging battle for market share on numerous routes. Fare wars broke out all over the country, as low-cost, low-fare, no-frills carriers like PeopleExpress began to get a toehold in major markets. Discounted fares became the major strategic thrust for everyone. Airlines either initiated the discounts or matched them. The discounting was so fast and furious that at one airline, the fare for a single-fare level on the New York–Fort Lauderdale route changed several times in just one day.

Travel agents were having a terrible time trying to keep up with all this. In some markets, the fares were so low that even if the planes were full—and most of them were—the airlines could not possibly make money. Traditional brand loyalty was a thing of the past, as customers ran from airline to airline to get the lowest fares in a market. Financial results in 1982 and 1983 were dismal; the established carriers were becoming deeply concerned.

In the postderegulation era, fare competition would obviously be a constant in the airline business. To find incremental revenue, Crandall turned his attention to discretionary travelers—customers who made their airline decision primarily on price, many of whom were choosing the new no-frills carriers. Determined that American would be in control of the discount fare game, Crandall and his team tackled the problem of how to compete effectively in the discount fare sector against all competitors, including carriers like PeopleExpress. The challenge was to maximize American's revenues in a multitiered industry, compete with all players, and still produce black ink at the end of the year.

But Crandall recognized that the fight for the discretionary customer would be difficult. By the end of 1983, American and the other big airlines discovered that the new entrants they had formerly ignored were starting to make significant inroads on their traditional turf—and not just the users of discount fares. In the uncertain economy of the early '80s, companies were discovering how to cut business travel expenses. Their executives were flying PeopleExpress.

PeopleExpress was moving in on several big markets, including the United/American stronghold New York–Chicago route. The two big carriers had managed to beat back the PeopleExpress challenge, but Crandall was clearly miffed. It was time to take on this upstart Burr and others like him on his own turf—the discount passenger market. With the combination of SABRE, the AAdvantage Frequent Flyer Program, and Yield Management, Crandall had just the strategic weapons he needed to do the job. Determined to come out on top, Crandall and several members of his inner circle embarked on an ultrasecret plan to recapture the momentum from the competition.

ATTACK OF THE LASER FARES

January 17, 1985, was shaping up to be Bob Crandall's kind of day. Then president of American Airlines, Crandall took off from Dallas and headed to New York. He was scheduled to address the elite Wings Club of aviation industry executives and analysts that afternoon. It was one of those clear, crisp, sunny winter days above the clouds—a beautiful day to fly. And Bob Crandall was flying high in more ways than one. By the time he got to New York, the *Wall Street Journal* would be announcing to the business world that he had been elected chairman and CEO of AMR, the parent company of American Airlines. It had been a long and difficult journey, but he had finally reached the pinnacle.

To add icing to the cake, the day would also bring another announcement of the kind that Bob Crandall loved. Early word of it had made the front page of the *Dallas Morning News,* and a press conference was scheduled for that afternoon. After months of tactical planning, American's carefully designed, ultrasecret discount fares plan would be launched. The plan was called Ultimate Super Savers, the discount fare package to end all discount fare packages. With Ultimate Super Savers, Crandall was single-handedly going to bring pricing sanity back to the airline industry, beat the crap out of the low-fare competition, and make money to boot. He was in full control, just the way he liked it. Yes, for Bob Crandall and American Airlines, it was going to be a beautiful day!

In New Jersey, at Newark International Airport, January 17, 1985, was one of those snowy, picturesque days that comes only a few times a winter. Donald Burr was heading to his office in the PeopleExpress terminal, and, like Crandall, the founder and president of PeopleExpress was riding high, although for different reasons. Coming off the most successful year in PeopleExpress's history, Burr had exciting plans for the airline. It had been an incredible year, but 1985 would be better. It might be snowing outside, but at PeopleExpress it was sunny.

But not for long. When Burr got to his office, the news of American's Ultimate Super Saver fares hit him like a sledge-hammer. American's discount fares were already scoring direct hits on PeopleExpress all over the country. The impact was devastating. PeopleExpress reeled from the blows as bookings began to fall and traffic disappeared. Burr couldn't believe it. What was happening? Confusion reigned. Phones rang off the hook as field offices all over the country reported the local effect of the new fares.

Frantically, Burr and his people tried to find out the details of American's attack plan. They called American reservations numbers in every city they served, trying to find out what markets were hit the hardest and where they were striking next. For the first time since PeopleExpress took to the air, they had reason to be scared.

Donald Burr says that he will never forget that fateful day in January 1985. What began as a routine winter day in New Jersey turned into a nightmare. "American took out full-page ads in every newspaper in the country," he remembers. "They had every one of our O&D's [origination/destination routes] listed, and it was our price or lower. *Every single one!* They were going to underprice PeopleExpress everywhere. Period. They were able to underprice us at will and *surreptitiously.* One second they would have the low price available and the next second they wouldn't have it.

"You could never tell where the hell they were killing you, except your load factors [percentage of seats filled] told you. Our load factors dropped almost in a straight line from 70%,

80%, and 90%, depending on the market, to 20%, 30%, and 40%." With a breakeven load factor (the point at which costs were covered) of about 61%, the company was in deep trouble.

Staggering from the immediate and devastating impact of American's fare missiles, Don Burr called his people together for an emergency meeting. "If we don't invent an answer to this, we're history," he told them. "We're going to be dead meat."

To the rest of the world, the launch of the Ultimate Super Savers looked like just another shot in the airline wars—another battle over a piece of turf. But something else was going on here. This was a new kind of engagement. This was a *secret* pricing war.

The secret weapon Crandall used wasn't a "gun" or "ammunition." Everyone in the industry had guns and ammo—

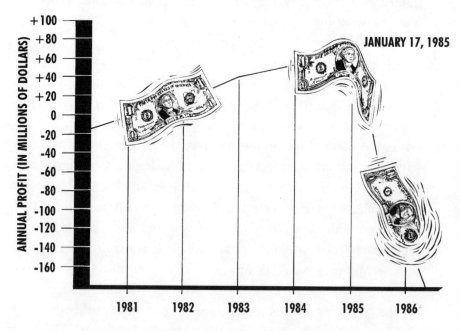

The Demise of PeopleExpress

automated reservations systems and discount fares. But with his unique combination of experience in information technology, finance, and marketing, Bob Crandall had envisioned a new way to outsmart the competition and win.

For over seven years, Crandall had been directing an effort at American Airlines to develop a new, automated guidance system that specified how much ammunition to put in the gun, where to aim it, and when to pull the trigger. Like the laser-guided missiles in the Gulf War, this secret weapon directed American's fare projectiles with computer-driven precision, zeroing in on specific micromarket targets all over the country and scoring on *every single launch!*

Back in Dallas, American's Yield Management department was in its own frenzy. This Ultimate Super Saver raid wasn't a "drop the bomb and run" deal. The job of the analysts was to continually reevaluate the situation, make sure they hit the target, and keep the pressure on. They didn't drop just one bomb. They dropped bombs all over the country, and they were still dropping them. This was really where the secret pricing war was being fought, and won.

American was still in the process of fine-tuning the secret weapon—the Yield Management guidance system—but by now it was fully operational. The system was ingenious. American would preserve its full-fare, bread-and-butter traffic; sell all of its surplus seats for incremental revenue; and effectively compete with every other airline in the country, including the low-fare, no-frills carriers like PeopleExpress.

The department was a beehive of energetic activity as American's Yield Management analysts, like traders in a commodity market, pecked away at computer terminals adding discount seats in this market and taking away discount seats in that market. But "it wasn't instantaneous enlightenment," recalls Barry Smith, who was in the middle of the action in Dallas. Although it was generally believed that American was way ahead of everyone else on Yield Management processes, it had never done anything like the Ultimate Super Savers before. It had no previous history to draw on for its forecasts.

"When those Ultimate Super Savers came out, they came out at a pretty high level within the company," remembers Smith. "I was in Yield Management and we were trying to figure out how to control the seats, because it was totally new. We had traffic and demand numbers from the previous season, but we didn't have anything that looked like this! I think that this was the first fare that had some nonrefundability associated with it. We didn't have any fares with that kind of restriction and we didn't have a clue [about this], so we were doing some really wild stuff out there just to get the allocations out." It was a learn-as-you-go situation. "It was a lot easier than it was at PeopleExpress obviously, but it had us scrambling around."

The panic wasn't confined to PeopleExpress. The rest of the airline industry was in an uproar too. Reeling from the shock of the Ultimate Super Saver announcement, most of American's competitors were scrambling to get on the bandwagon as fast as they could. While pricing departments hurriedly assembled competitive fare packages, industry executives decried the fares, screaming that they would erode profit potential. American countered by saying that if the company didn't believe it could make money with the Ultimate Super Savers, it wouldn't offer them. American tried to explain that the fares were part of an overall fares restructuring plan, but the competition wasn't buying it.

WALL STREET REACTS

The fares restructuring explanation also didn't wash with Wall Street analysts that January day. They blasted American, saying that the Ultimate Super Savers were just an aggressive attempt to muscle weaker carriers out of American's markets and fuel its own expansion. Wall Street had no knowledge of American's secret weapon and its new approach to targeted discounts. To Wall Street, this was a suicidal fare war.

When Bob Crandall got off the plane at La Guardia that morning, he learned that while he was in the air between Dallas and New York, all hell had broken loose on the AMR stock at the New York Stock Exchange. When the Ultimate Super Saver news had hit that morning, stockbrokers were inundated with sell orders for AMR. The pressure to sell was so intense that traders couldn't find enough buyers to take the dumped AMR shares. The exchange finally suspended trading on AMR for three hours at $32\frac{1}{4}$—a whopping 13% drop in one day. The fallout continued the next day, when analysts pounded American again in the same newspapers that carried the first Ultimate Super Saver ads. Without any knowledge of Yield Management and its ability to maximize revenues while still offering discount fares, the analysts questioned the wisdom of setting off yet another fare war. Wall Street just didn't get it, but for competitive reasons, Crandall wasn't about to tell the world about his new secret weapon.

Donald Burr and his cohorts hoped that there would be backlash from the public. They mistakenly believed that the public would not tolerate variable prices on the same airplane. "We kept saying that the customers won't put up with this," recalls Burr. "They will revolt. American's not going to be able to do it. The government won't let American and United do this."

They thought the government wouldn't allow what Burr and his colleagues considered to be bait-and-switch pricing because of the limited availability of the low fares offered. They just couldn't believe that the $1,000 passenger would tolerate sitting next to the $100 passenger on the same airplane. They were wrong.

Smelling blood, the other major airlines jumped into the fray as fast as they could. After six years of deregulation, they knew they had to make a stand on every discount fare that came into the market, especially if the discount fares were launched by a giant like American. Most of the airlines had reservations systems sophisticated enough to provide the data needed to manipulate seat inventories by different fare classes. Most of them had been practicing some form of Yield Management with varying degrees of success for a couple of years. They had to protect their turf. Besides, they also saw this turn of events as an opportunity to get back the customers they had lost to PeopleExpress and the other discount carriers.

At American Airlines, the Yield Management group was still course correcting. Phil Haan, now senior vice president for international at Northwest Airlines, was at American at the time and remembers how the yield managers responded. "We chose initially not to allow more than 50% of the seats on any particular flight to be in the Ultimate Super Savers category. There were generous amounts of availability, but we capped every flight. It turned out to be more constraining than we wanted, and it took a while for us to come to grips with adding lots more discount seats. We ended up going through this long time period where salespeople started going into SABRE and capturing booking information on their own. They'd discover a flight that went out with forty-two empty seats, so we in Yield Management would get a lot of pressure. But nobody would give you pressure when the flight went out 99% full and you sold too many of the discounts."

The experience caused American to install more management information systems to understand product availability—both how much product American had available and how much the competitors had available. There was a lot of skepticism about seat inventory controls in the marketplace at the time, Haan remembers. "People would say that the Ultimate Super Saver fare offering was only fluff and that we were really only putting one seat on every plane at the discount fare. PeopleExpress was calling it a bait-and-switch game and we would find that infuriating . . . because we knew that 40% to 80% of our flights would easily have almost unlimited discount availability."

While its Yield Management capabilities were way ahead of those of the other airlines in 1985, American still had a long way to go to reach revenue maximization. Dinamo was still a couple of years away, and the Yield Management personnel were essentially working with systems that had been in place for a number of years. American's technology was still rudimentary, but what it had was enough to make Ultimate Super Savers not only successful tactically but highly profitable.

AFTERMATH

In the weeks that followed American's Ultimate Super Saver bombing, almost every newspaper in the country was full of discount fare ads. Meanwhile, Don Burr was feeling the heat. His old boss at Texas International, Frank Lorenzo, had acquired Continental Airlines, and he was leading the horde of competitors, going after the embattled PeopleExpress with ads that showed no mercy. The headline of one read, "Continental Takes the People Out of PeopleExpress," and that's exactly what Lorenzo intended to do.

Airline customers voted with their feet. Weary of the hassles of flying with PeopleExpress and the dingy Newark terminal, they lined up to buy the limited discount seats offered by American, United, Continental, Delta, and others. They wanted to make a reservation and be reasonably assured that their seat wouldn't be sold to someone else before they got to the airport. They wanted to buy their tickets from their in-town travel agents. They wanted to check their luggage and find it waiting for them, undamaged, at the end of the flight. They wanted a soft drink or a hot meal without paying extra to get it. And, now, they could get it all on American Airlines for the same cheap price, or less, than they had been paying PeopleExpress. All this and frequent-flier points too!

Virtually overnight, PeopleExpress planes were flying almost empty. For Donald Burr and his company, the game was now one of survival. It would take some dramatic moves for PeopleExpress to recover from American's devastating blow and regain its profitable position. Don Burr was willing to do whatever it would take. He might be down, but he wasn't out yet.

Critical mass was then the name of the game, and Burr believed that the airline would have to grow quickly to survive. PeopleExpress went into a growth frenzy. Burr bought Denver-based Frontier Airlines, overhauled its reservations system, instituted rudimentary Yield Management tactics, and began inaugurating new domestic routes as fast as he could get airplanes to fly them. He bought Britt Airways and Provincetown-Boston Airlines in the first half of 1986. By then, the growth was badly straining the infrastructure of the company. By June 1986, PeopleExpress was serving 158 airports and carrying over one million passengers a month. In a few short years, it had leaped to the number five spot in the airline hierarchy, after United, American, Delta, and Eastern, all of which had been in business at least fifty years more than PeopleExpress.

Don Burr had forced the industry into the discount fares business in a big way. Now, using the emerging science of Revenue Management, the major airlines, led by American, had mastered the discount fares business in a way that Burr had never envisioned. Now, *they* were forcing *him* to change.

Don Burr made several last-ditch attempts to save his company. In a complete turnabout, he tried to re-create PeopleExpress as a full-service airline, which required installing first-class sections and constructing VIP lounges all over the system. It was a bold idea, but this totally new direction was counter to everything PeopleExpress had stood for since the day it had started flying. The public didn't buy it, and by now it was too late. The death spiral was too far along to reverse. Ironically, Burr was forced to sell his company to his old boss, Frank Lorenzo, now head of the newly resuscitated Continental Airlines and a bitter rival.

The PeopleExpress odyssey came to an end on September 15, 1986. To Burr, it marked the death of a dream. "We were a vibrant, profitable company from 1981 to 1985, and then we tipped right over into losing $50 million a month. We were still the same company. Still at Newark. There were no changes in this company. What changed was American's ability to do widespread Yield Management in every one of our markets. We had been profitable from the day we started until American came at us with Ultimate Super Savers. That was the end of our run because they were able to underprice us at will, and surreptitiously. There was nothing left to defend us.

"All we had left was our cost structure, which at the time was a billion dollars a year less than American. You figure that at a billion dollars cheaper, you ought to be safe. We kept naively hoping that our billion-dollar cushion would give us enough room even if they underpriced us here and there. But all they needed to take away from us was that marginal traffic above breakeven. You don't have to take away half the guy's market. All you have to do is take away a few seats on every flight and the guy's dead."

CRANDALL'S VINDICATION

American's financial report at the end of 1985 vindicated Bob Crandall. There was no doubt that Crandall had scored big with the Ultimate Super Saver launch. The airline's traffic in January 1985 had grown by over 15% to 3.1 billion revenue passenger miles (one paying passenger flown one mile) from the same month in 1984. With the control of discount fare inventories, a strike by United pilots, and more favorable fuel prices, American reported a net profit of $345.8 million for the year, up 47.8% from 1984, while its revenue increased 14.5% to $6.1 billion.

In the eyes of his employees, Crandall confirmed his reputation as a fierce competitor at the 1987 American Airlines sales meeting in Fort Worth, Texas. Dressed in military camouflage fatigues, a guerrilla bandanna on his head, and a simulated attack rifle in his hand, Crandall made his video debut as "Crando," the terror of the competition and the unrelenting battle machine in the airline wars.

Crandall denies that American was specifically targeting PeopleExpress on January 17, 1985. "The answer is no. If you set out to put somebody else out of business, what you're probably going to do is inflict terrible damage on yourself.

What we were trying to do then was to prevent *them* from putting *us* out of business.

"Really what happened was that we had empty seats. Because we had other revenues on the airplane, the residual cost of those seats was less than the full cost of PeopleExpress seats. If we could figure out a way to fill them at People-Express prices, our margins on those seats were higher than PeopleExpress margins on its universe of seats available at that price."

No one is more qualified to attest to the value of Yield Management than Bob Crandall. He was among the first to recognize the rationale for developing such systems, and he saw to it that American's developmental teams had management support for their endeavors. "I believe that Yield Management is the single most important technical development in transportation management since we entered the era of airline deregulation in 1979," says Crandall. "The development of

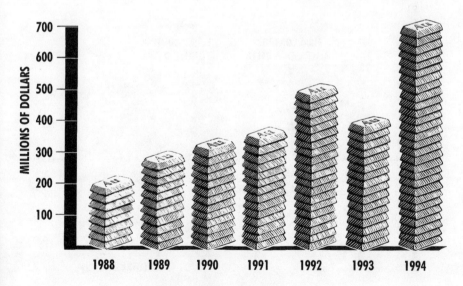

Incremental Revenue from RM at American Airlines
SOURCE: AMERICAN AIRLINES

Yield Management was a key to American Airlines's survival in the postderegulation environment. We expect Yield Management to generate at least $500 million annually for the foreseeable future."

Another way to measure the effect of Revenue Management is by comparing the performance of the major airlines when the Ultimate Super Savers were launched. In the first quarter of 1985, the Ultimate Super Saver fares significantly stimulated U.S. airline traffic. Traffic grew 13.2%, while total industry revenues grew 6.2%. At the time of the Ultimate Super Saver war, the airlines had varying degrees of Revenue Management capability, ranging from sophisticated (for the time) to no controls at all. The airlines that were the most advanced in their implementation of Revenue Management tactics were American and Delta. Collectively, these two saw a traffic gain of 15% and increased their revenues 9% in the first quarter. United and TWA, by contrast, had made little

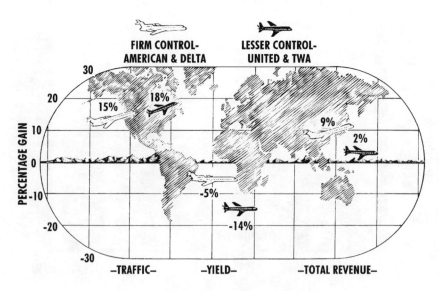

Ultimate Super Saver Results

progress with RM at the time. Collectively, their revenue rose only 2% despite a traffic gain of 18% by the two carriers.

POSTSCRIPT

Don Burr is now living in a comfortable New England home on the ocean at Martha's Vineyard. Since 1987, he has been a sought-after speaker and has served as a guest lecturer at Harvard Business School. He also consults with groups of investors who contemplate starting airlines. Burr believes that the critical mistake he made was failing to develop a vision of the role that information technology could play in the airline business.

"Obviously, PeopleExpress failed," admits Burr. "We're not around any more. We had great people, tremendous value, terrific growth. We did a lot of things right. But we didn't get our hands around the Yield Management and automation issues." If PeopleExpress had invested in a more comprehensive reservations system in 1981, it most likely would have had the database needed to install Revenue Management processes to fight American's Ultimate Super Saver assault.

Burr is a big believer in the power of information technology and Revenue Management. If he were starting an airline today, he says, "I guess the number one priority on my list every day would be to see that my people got the best possible information technology tools. In my view, that's what drives airline revenues today more than any other factor—more than service, more than planes, more than routes. Traffic on the margin is driven by the best use of information technology."

Burr also likes to tell a story about the real moment he

knew he was in trouble. "It was Thanksgiving of 1985. I'll never forget it. My mother called and said she was going to take American Airlines to visit my brother. American Airlines was almost giving away seats throughout the entire country to put a sharp exclamation point on their claim that American would not be undersold by anyone, anywhere. The public knew instantly on Thanksgiving of 1985 that they could get from American, at our price or better, *everything* American had to offer."

Goliath's triumph was complete.

The RM Revolution

We work hard to save money in costs and to operate more efficiently; but frankly, it's so much easier to make a buck doing Revenue Management.
—RICHARD FAIN, CHAIRMAN AND CEO,
ROYAL CARIBBEAN CRUISE LINES

DOES RM APPLY TO YOUR BUSINESS?

MOST BUSINESSES ARE CONtinually seeking new solutions to the issues that plague them: demanding consumers, impatient investors, tough competitors, and information overload. The solutions they have employed may have helped, but they are often painful and usually don't address all the issues. I am sure this is why I am often called upon to speak before diverse groups of businesspeople about RM concepts. Once they hear some of the extraordinary success stories involving Revenue Management, one of the first questions they have is: "Does RM apply to my business?"

I remind my questioners of the definition of RM: the application of disciplined tactics that predict consumer behavior at the micromarket level and optimize product price and availability for the purpose of maximizing revenue growth—selling the right product to the right customer at the right time for the right price. Most people then realize that this concept applies to virtually all businesses. They all have "products," which have some perceived value to their customers. There is not an unlimited supply of the product, nor is there unlimited demand, and there are always alternatives from competitors.

Therefore, businesses must make numerous decisions about the pricing and availability of their products to the marketplace. These decisions can be made in an ad hoc way or at various levels of sophistication. The important thing is to recognize the kind of decisions you are making and to employ the right level of analysis and effort to the decision-making process.

I occasionally encounter resistance to adopting RM techniques and using computers for managing and making critical marketing decisions. A few years ago, the information services director of a large cruise line invited me to make a presentation on Revenue Management to the president of his company. I explained the basic concepts and how they applied to the cruise industry, and I used a PC to demonstrate one version of an RM system. At the end of the meeting, he cordially thanked me for coming but said, "Revenue Management isn't for us. This is not the way we want to manage our markets, and we're just not into using computers for this kind of thing." Before giving up, I decided to ask him a couple of questions.

"How many cruise berths do you sell a week?" I asked.

"About ten to twelve thousand."

"You do discount your cabins, don't you?"

"Absolutely. If we didn't, we'd be sailing empty. The competition is incredible."

"In peak periods, you discount less, don't you?"

"Sure. We'd be stupid to give it away."

"How do you decide how many berths to discount and how deeply to discount them?"

"We meet every Monday morning and look at the advance bookings for future sailings and, as a management team, decide the discount levels."

"You don't understand," I told him. "You are already practicing Revenue Management, but you're doing it in a shoot-from-the-hip fashion. You're relying on personal observation and intuition to manage the price and availability of 520,000 berths over the course of next year. Yet, bookings are changing daily and competitors are constantly making pricing and product moves. All I'm talking about is a much more sophisticated and accurate way to improve what you are already doing."

The producers of all goods and services must understand their products and markets so that they can maximize their return from those assets. The savvy ones will not be satisfied with operating on an ad hoc basis. They will always be looking for a way to improve their ability to perform efficiently and profitably.

RM techniques can apply to virtually any commercial endeavor, but a sophisticated program is not necessarily called for in all cases. Over the years, my firm has become increasingly involved with companies that employ high-powered RM techniques. But RM is effective at any level because it can be used to reduce uncertainty in decision making by understanding and predicting customer behavior at the micromarket level. By converting uncertainty to probability, you can make better judgments about the price and availability of your products in the various market segments.

THE SEVEN UNCERTAINTIES

RM techniques certainly can't address all the difficult questions facing business leaders. But RM is adept at improving certain kinds of decision making. To judge the applicability of RM, a manager should begin with an assessment of seven uncertainties in the marketplace. The extent to which a company or enterprise encounters several or all of these uncertainties, as well as the degree of challenge it faces in each, forms the basis for understanding how useful RM will be. It will also assist in the development of appropriate tools and processes.

THE SEVEN UNCERTAINTIES

1. Perishable products and opportunities
2. Seasonal and other demand peaks
3. The product's value in different market segments
4. Product wastage
5. Competition between individual and bulk purchasers
6. Discounting to meet competition
7. Rapidly changing circumstances

PERISHABLE PRODUCTS AND OPPORTUNITIES

Selling perishable products presents a major revenue risk to companies that deal with them. RM techniques can help reduce the uncertainty about the demand for those products and reduce the risk of leaving them unsold. The problem of perishability of valuable assets was at the origin of RM. You can't sell an empty seat on an airplane that has already taken off. You can't sell last night's empty hotel room, nor can you sell the unsold TV commercial spot after the program airs. In all these cases, the asset the company has to sell is eliminated by the passage of time.

Many businesses and enterprises deal with such perishable assets. Restaurants have table times they must efficiently use. If a table is empty at the peak lunch hour, a revenue-generating opportunity has expired forever. Hospitals have operating rooms with "slots" for surgery that expire hourly. Telecommunications companies have network capacity that they either use or lose. For lawyers, accountants, and consultants, their perishable asset is their time. If they do not use their time today to generate revenues, that opportunity is gone tomorrow. In all these cases, the asset for sale has value one moment, but at the next, it is gone. This creates an urgent need to ensure that those assets are utilized effectively.

For many products, the perishability is literal. Items such as milk, bread, eggs, and fresh fruits and vegetables don't perish instantly if unsold, but they do have a definite period within which they will perish. Other products such as candy, vitamins, and drugs may have expiration dates at which they must be removed from the shelves. In such cases, the need to sell a product before it perishes is easy to understand, but solving the dilemma is no less difficult. How often have you gone to a supermarket or deli at the end of the day and seen a tray of potato salad destined to be thrown away and wondered how the store can afford to waste it this way?

A concept that is less clear to business is that of *perishable opportunity*. In many businesses, the physical product does not perish, but the opportunity to sell it for full price does. This week's issue of *Sports Illustrated* or *Time* magazine does not perish next week, but the opportunity to sell it at retail does. A Dallas Cowboys Super Bowl sweatshirt doesn't wither and disappear two months after the team wins the Super Bowl, but the chance to sell it for full price does as the product moves through its value cycle. Kittens and puppies in pet stores are more valuable before they become cats and dogs. This concept of perishability of opportunity extends to almost any business—real estate, retail sales, and manufacturing are all affected by the concept of perishable opportunities. If the timing isn't right, the opportunity to get the most out of the product will perish.

Fashion is a good example. Many consumers pay dearly for fashion. But fashion wears out faster than clothes do. Consumers will pay a premium for a fashionable piece of clothing, but once the item is no longer in style, its value diminishes significantly. Last season's clothes are heavily discounted. Many other consumer goods are also tied to the concept of fashion. When Dolly Parton's line of cosmetics first came out, it sold in department stores for $89.95. Eventually, it was relegated to the discount bins for $1.99.

Companies committed to maximizing revenues must predict consumer behavior in advance and respond while the product still has value. This can be done with a simple no-tech approach. Boston's Filene's Basement, for example, reduces the price for leftover merchandise incrementally over a thirty-five-day period until it sells. If it's not sold when the price is reduced by 75%, they give it away to charity. This is almost a reverse auction, where the store owner bids the price down until it is sold. Other retailers do this on an ad hoc basis with respect to perishable foodstuffs, but typically they wait until the product is almost valueless and then impose drastic price cuts. A revenue-maximizing firm would use RM techniques to forecast the declining value of its product with more precision and price it accordingly. The degree of sophistication of Revenue Management required is a function of the value of a product and the speed of its perishability. Maximizing the return from eighty thousand Super Bowl tickets requires a higher level of RM sophistication than does an equal number of Super Bowl sweatshirts.

RM TACTICS

These RM tactics help you maximize revenue when you have perishable products or opportunities:

- Use price balancing.
- Maximize revenue through optimal timing.

SEASONAL AND OTHER DEMAND PEAKS

Uncertainties caused by seasonal or other demand imbalances can also play havoc with a company's ability to maximize revenues and profits. Many companies face various seasonal peaks and valleys throughout the course of a year. Accounting firms, for example, have tremendous seasonal fluctuations. They are extremely busy during tax season. Other businesses have peaks around holiday periods such as Christmas. Retailers and catalog firms are typical examples. These firms commonly add supplementary staff and work many hours of overtime during the peak season. For some businesses, the demand peaks occur at much shorter intervals. For example, restaurants and theaters peak on weekends. They, too, usually staff for peaks either through adding people or incurring overtime.

Other firms may have significant off-peak periods. These periods can either be seasonal, such as those experienced by theme parks, or by day of week, such as automobile dealers whose workload falls dramatically during the week. Most companies try to lower costs in the off-peaks by reducing capacity, laying off staff, or borrowing money to tide them over. These are all examples of using capital, not price, to balance supply and demand. These are not necessarily improper responses to the marketplace, but they may not be optimal.

Revenue-driven corporations, on the other hand, are always alert to any opportunity to use market-based pricing, rather than capital, to take advantage of demand fluctuations. Under the right circumstances, discounts can be offered to attract customers or to entice them to move to the less popular times. This can help generate incremental revenue without disrupting the workforce. In addition, price increases or premiums can be used as a mechanism to shift demand to the off-peak or generate additional revenue from peak periods where adding capacity is impractical or inefficient. Shifting demand is what Carol Meinke successfully did in her one-chair barbershop.

Jonathan Carmel, former administrative director of Duke University Medical Center's Diet and Fitness Center, pioneered the first known formal use of RM principles in the health care industry in 1992. Duke's Diet and Fitness center (DFC) is one of three major diet facilities located in Durham, North Carolina. Over two thousand people visit Durham annually to lose weight. DFC's maximum capacity at the time was 140 patients, and the twenty-eight-day average program was priced at $4,200. Clients ranged from middle-class men and women to millionaires, and from young singles wanting to lose a few pounds before swimsuit season to middle-aged executives trying to work off the accumulation of power lunches and dinners.

The holiday-oriented months of November and December were the traditional off-peak months during which the center was losing up to $75,000 a month. There might be only twenty or thirty clients booked during these months, but fixed costs stayed the same. To stimulate the market in the off-peak periods, Carmel dropped the regular rate by 25%, which doubled the number of patients. The increased revenue not only reversed his losses, it delivered a profit of $5,000–$10,000 a month.

The success of this simple pricing experiment led Carmel to closely examine the rates for the peak times, when the center routinely turned away excess demand. After careful analysis, Carmel increased peak summer rates by 15%–20% and then offered clients a 15% discount if they booked sixty days in advance. This is classic Revenue Management. Not only did Carmel achieve his goal of spreading out the demand, he still got premium prices during the peak season and served more clients. More important, he *increased overall annual revenue by 10%!*

These tactics could be applied to other aspects of the health care field. Weekday mornings are peak times for operating room theaters. Demand for expensive equipment such as X-ray machines, magnetic resonance imaging (MRI) equipment, and high-dose radiation therapy equipment peaks between 8:00 A.M. and 5:00 P.M. on weekdays, while they sit virtually idle at night and on weekends. RM techniques could help spread the demand for these valuable resources and make more efficient utilization of them by segmenting the market and charging more during the peaks and discounting during the off-peak.

Other firms are experimenting with the concept of using market-based pricing to balance supply and demand. In Atlanta, the accountants at Coopers & Lybrand charge a slight premium for work done in the peak tax period, and they offer a discount for accounting services performed in the off-peak. Not only does this enhance revenues during the peak period, it encourages clients to use the firm's time wisely during the hectic tax season. This practice also enables clients to receive discounts on other accounting services if they are willing to request them when the firm has spare capacity.

Instead of simply using price alone to optimize scarce resources and level out peak and off-peak demand, some companies use a combination of pricing and inventory control. The Marriott Corporation has been a leader in this field. A focus on revenue has always been a part of the Marriott culture, and it's no surprise that Marriott spearheaded the application of Revenue Management techniques in the hotel business.

As with many hotel firms that target business travelers, most Marriott hotels have peak days during the middle of the week. Marriott has had an RM system that can maximize the revenue for any given night for several years, but Rich Hanks, senior vice president of sales, felt that Marriott hotels were still missing a revenue opportunity. Accepting a guest who stayed only on the peak Wednesday night, for example, often meant turning away guests who might have stayed longer. Hanks thought it could be more profitable to accept longer-stay guests, even at a lower rate, especially if this helped fill those "shoulder" periods that surround peak demand times.

Some Marriott hotels had attempted this tactic on an ad hoc basis. Hanks ordered a simulation study on a more sophisticated approach. The study showed that it was possible to forecast the guest demand both by price and length of stay for every hotel fairly accurately. Using these forecasts of customer behavior could generate between $25 million and $35 million in annual incremental revenue. Encouraged by the study, Hanks oversaw the development of a computer system called DFS (Demand Forecasting System) that dynamically forecasts guest arrival, departure, and price patterns. Based on the forecasted guest activity, which is reviewed and revised daily, DFS recommended rates and length-of-stay restrictions. The DFS concept was met with some skepticism, especially from some of the "old-timers" who felt that either guest behavior could not be predicted or, if it could be, they could do better than the machine.

But testing made believers out of just about everyone. One of the test sites for DFS was the Munich Marriott during Oktoberfest. The conventional wisdom embraced by all the hotels in the area was that it was best to eliminate any discount rates whatsoever during this period because of the tremendous demand. DFS, however, recommended that the hotel offer some rooms at a discount, but only for those guests who would stay for an extended period either before or after the peak days of the celebration. While this was counter to what the general manager felt was "common sense," he applied this recommendation anyway. At the end of Oktoberfest, he was delighted with the results. Although the average daily rate was down 11.7% for the period, occupancy was up over 20% and overall revenues were up 12.3%. DFS was used to dynamically forecast customer demand at the micromarket level to employ demand-based pricing and to save rooms for the highest-value guests.

Marriott has pioneered many such Revenue Management concepts in the hotel industry and continues to look for revenue improvements. "When you focus on the bottom line, you grow," explains Bill Marriott, chairman and CEO of Marriott International. "We're continually challenging our people to open their minds and think outside the box."

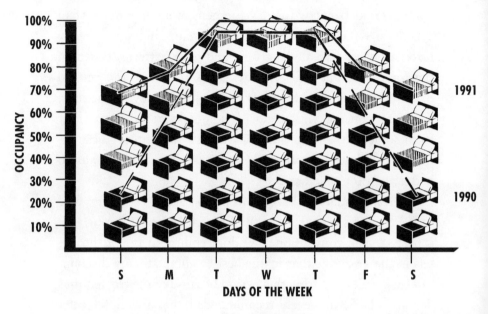

RM at Oktoberfest

RM TACTICS

These RM tactics best help you address seasonal or other demand peaks in your business:

- Use price balancing.
- Forecast at the micromarket level.

THE PRODUCT'S VALUE IN DIFFERENT MARKET SEGMENTS

RM techniques are especially useful in dealing with the opportunities presented by the variance in values that your product represents to different customer segments. Certain customers will value your product more than other customers, and, accordingly, they are willing to pay more.

Some of the customers at Carol's barbershop valued the convenience of a Saturday haircut more than a few extra dollars. For many people, a night at the theater on Friday or Saturday is more valuable than on a night during the week. Consumers are willing to pay more for a product that they perceive has greater value, but often businesses don't capture this difference between a customer's perception of value and the price they charge. This difference is lost to the business forever. The difference between what consumers are willing to pay and what they actually pay is called "consumer surplus." A great example is Super Bowl tickets. The average price for Super Bowl XXX tickets was $250 if purchased from the National Football League. But the going rate for Super Bowl tickets in the secondary market was $1,450, giving the people who were able to purchase tickets directly an average consumer surplus of $1,200.

This consumer surplus costs businesses billions of dollars a year. For many businesses, survival or failure may depend on their ability to identify these lost opportunities and capture the consumer surplus. Take PC manufacturer Packard Bell. It captured the lead in home computer market share through aggressive discounting but was struggling financially in mid-1996. Whatever its other problems, Packard Bell almost certainly has a pricing problem. From an RM perspective, it seems to be offering discounts that are too large to too many micromarkets. If Packard Bell could reduce this apparent consumer surplus, consumers might pay a little more in the short term, but consumers would have the long-term benefit of keeping a viable competitor in the market.

Businesses must be equally attuned to instances in which they can expand their markets by offering target discounts to certain market segments. PC manufacturers, for example, could offer deep discounts to job training programs. The consumers in these instances will directly benefit from the price reductions targeted to them.

For many businesses, this sort of market-based pricing, based on variances in perceived value, will take no more than astute observation and a willingness to shift thinking. Take restaurants, for example. The patrons who dine on Friday and Saturday night at first-rate restaurants are typically willing to pay more than those who dine during the week, since the Friday night meal is often considered part of an evening's entertainment and not just the taking of sustenance. But most restaurants don't charge more for a Friday or Saturday night even though customers may perceive a greater value. By the same token, they don't charge less for a weeknight when the perceived value is lower. In both cases, the restaurants may miss revenue opportunities—from charging more on weekends and from generating additional business on weekdays. The Revenue Management techniques used in these circumstances could be as basic as those Carol applied at her barbershop.

But not all situations are so simple. Computer chip makers face the dilemma of having many consumers who place a wide range of value on their products. Demand is booming for semiconductors such as memory chips and microprocessors. According to Dataquest, global sales of all types of semiconductors rose in 1995 by 40% to $155 billion. Chip makers are astute enough not to engage in cost-plus pricing. However, for the most part, they do not understand the price/value tradeoffs that their customers must make. This is partly because in most cases they are one step removed from the ultimate consumer—the buyer of the PC. The demand varies according to the nature of the chip—that is, whether it is a CPU chip, a customized logic chip, or a memory chip. Demand also varies depending on the chip's functionality and performance. For CPU chips, some customers are willing to pay a significant premium for maximum performance, even if it doesn't seem to be cost-justifiable. For example, a chip maker could conceivably charge twice as much for a newly introduced 200-megahertz chip as for a widely available 150-megahertz chip, even though the faster chip offers only a 25% improvement in performance. The question of how high a premium to charge for a new chip is a classic Revenue Management problem that could be addressed by analyzing all transactions and performing price sensitivity analysis. The chip-making business is now so large that it would take only a 1% improvement in pricing to generate over $1.5 billion in incremental revenues for the industry.

RM techniques could also assist the semiconductor industry with the timing of the introduction of new chips. Using the rocket launch analogy, each new chip could be considered a separate "stage" where revenue trajectory was forecast and optimized, and new products could be launched at the optimal point to maximize revenues.

Understanding the variance in values that your product represents is vital in the amoeba market. Yet a lot of companies stop at the first step—the actual value of the product to them—because they either don't realize that consumers may value their products differently or have not figured out a way to determine the perceived value of their products to the multiplying micromarkets.

RM TACTICS

Three RM tactics best help you deal with the differences in how market segments value your products:

- •Use market-based pricing.
- •Use segment pricing.
- •Forecast at the micromarket level.

PRODUCT WASTAGE

Product wastage is an enormous thief of revenue opportunity. The concept is similar to that of perishability of product or opportunity, but with a distinction. Perishable products expire when you don't sell them. Product wastage as defined by RM occurs when a product is reserved, or sold in advance, but in the end the sale does not go through and cannot be recovered. This is a familiar issue with airlines. They may have sold out a flight, but no-show passengers make the flight depart with empty seats. No-shows cost the world's airlines over $3 billion annually, even after efforts to minimize the revenue loss by overbooking. Without overbooking, the loss would be tens of billions of dollars.

Hotels have a similar problem with no-shows; in addition, they must cope with guests who check out before the end of their expected stay. Restaurants also struggle with the no-show issue when they take reservations. Some restaurants, for example, may experience a no-show rate as high as 30% on holidays, when the opportunity for income is highest. To counter the problem, some restaurants are experimenting with cancellation fees charged to credit cards that are used to guarantee the reservation.

Manufacturers may also reserve significant productive capacity for a certain customer and lose the opportunity to resell that capacity at the same rate if the customer cancels or delays a major order. Cancellation fees, the traditional hedge against this problem, seldom make up for the lost revenue. Doctors, hair salons, automakers, cabinetmakers, architects, and any other business that accepts reservations for future delivery of goods and services face the same issue. Fear of the no-show problem prevented Carol from even considering taking reservations in her barbershop. In most cases, cancellation fees are either not appropriate or do not sufficiently offset the cost of the no-show. If a business arbitrarily overbooks time slots to protect against this wastage, it risks having more customers show up than it can possibly serve. If it doesn't overbook and there are significant no-shows, the business will hope for walk-up demand or beat the bushes to make up the lost revenue.

What makes overbooking under such circumstances so risky is that the no-shows will vary by product and micromarket, making it even more difficult to forecast customer behavior and optimize your response. For example, a rental car firm's no-show rate will vary depending upon day of week, customer type (business versus leisure), car type, season, and geographic location. This requires detailed forecasting and optimization at the micromarket level.

Some companies face a similar issue when they guarantee the repurchase of unsold goods from their retail outlets. Magazine and book publishers frequently allow retailers to return unsold products that cannot be resold or must be sold at drastically reduced prices. Bakeries are also hurt by this sort of product wastage. The attempted turnaround effort at a large bakery in the Midwest is a case in point. The turnaround specialist noticed that the company was losing lots of money from absorbing the cost of wastage when unsold bread was brought back from the retail stores. He thought that a computer model could do a better job of forecasting demand than the route salespeople, who were obviously leaving too much product at the stores. The computer model, however, ended up causing even greater losses. Although the model did a better job of forecasting overall demand, it was not designed to account for all the differences at the micro-market level, based on product type, day of week, and the individual location of the retail store. This resulted in not having the right product at the right store at the right time. So, by averaging demand across too many variables, the model ended up shipping too much of one product to one location and too little to another. In this situation, the route salespeople had done a better job than the computer model because they knew of these micromarket distinctions and had tried to take them into consideration on a case-by-case basis. The information available to the salespeople at the micromarket level was better than the aggregated data used by the computer model.

Understanding and gaining control of product wastage requires analysis at the micromarket level. The sophisticated forecasting tools of RM have helped many companies significantly reduce product wastage and reap the revenue benefits from selling more of their available inventory before it expires.

RM TACTICS

Product wastage can be minimized using these RM tactics:

- Forecast at the micromarket level.
- Maximize revenue through optimal timing.

COMPETITION BETWEEN INDIVIDUAL
AND BULK PURCHASERS

Most companies face price/volume trade-offs and competition between individual and bulk purchasers for the exact same product or set of products. Customers who buy single units or small lots generally pay higher per-unit prices, whereas bulk purchasers usually buy large volumes of a company's products or services at substantial discounts. This creates the classic confrontation between price and volume. Bob McKenna, who held senior executive positions at Avis, Hertz, and National Car Rental, relates a story that illustrates a problem familiar to many companies. "The sales executive for a rental car business comes into the Monday morning staff meeting proudly announcing that he just won the IBM contract! This is something he and his people have been working on for years. They stole the account from under the noses of their greatest rival, and, given a recent dip in retail demand, the timing couldn't be better. A celebration breaks out, champagne is poured, cheers and high-fives all around. It's a great day!

"Within weeks, however, they discover the true cost—much of their capacity is committed throughout the year at a very low rate. Retail demand for their cars picks up later in the year, and soon everyone is asking 'How much longer do we have to go on that damned IBM contract?' "

So, to whom do you sell your product—individual or bulk purchasers? And at what price and under what circumstances do you sell it to them? Some firms, like sports teams and performing arts organizations, try to sell as much inventory as they can up front at a bulk rate to bring revenue in the door as soon as possible. Season tickets, for example, usually cost less per individual event than tickets purchased at the door. This is basically the "bird in the hand is worth more than two in the bush" philosophy, which is fine, provided that the organization fully understands the impact of this practice on revenue maximization. But what if the inventory being sold up front at volume discounts could be sold later to individual buyers at a much higher unit price? Should you take the risk that there will, in fact, be enough individual customers who will purchase the product later?

According to the *Wall Street Journal,* in 1995 the major TV networks sold over 90% of their prime ad spots in the "up-front" market. The networks were crowing that they pulled in a record $5.77 billion in commitments and that the percentage of up-front commitments was higher than ever. (Networks typically sell about 80% of the upcoming season's ads in the up-front market.) Still, one of the TV executives mentioned that when they sell the remaining spots individually in the "scatter market" later in the season they often get as much as 45% more per spot. So did it really make sense to sell almost all of the ad spots up front? The powerful demand-forecasting tools, processes, and systems of RM could answer this difficult question and maximize the return. Given that a major network has fifteen thousand to twenty thousand spots to manage and sell over the course of a year, forecasting the ever-changing demand and value of those spots as the season progresses would require an enormous amount of data and constant analysis. But it can be done.

The application of Revenue Management concepts to the problem of striking a balance between bulk and individual purchasers can also be done on a no-tech or low-tech scale. The issues are the same: forecast the demand for the higher-value sales and discount only those that you need to fill your capacity. Commercial real estate firms, for instance, must balance the value a large tenant is willing to pay, say, $20 a square foot, versus a number of smaller ones willing to pay $25 a square foot. Basic low-tech RM applications can help a company selling commercial real estate figure out how to allocate its product appropriately.

RM Tactics

If competition between individual and bulk purchasers is a factor in your business, try the following RM tactics:

- Use segment pricing.
- Favor the most valuable customers.

DISCOUNTING TO MEET COMPETITION

None of the issues we've discussed—demand pricing, variable pricing, and saving assets for high-valued users—can be done in isolation. Competition will certainly affect, if not drive, your reaction in the marketplace. Competitor-initiated price discounting is an almost universal problem.

Price discounting can arise even in the most unusual quarters. In 1992, the prostitutes of Biella, Italy, faced an unprecedented problem when immigrant hookers invaded their market. To gain market share in a hurry, the immigrant hookers undercut the agreed rates of the Biella call girls, taking substantial business away in short order. The Biella prostitutes offered clients free services to regain lost business. This was a costly overreaction to the need to meet competition. The Biella group could have made money by correctly segmenting their market to compete with the low-cost competition in the price-sensitive segment and retained their price-insensitive repeat customers.

Winning price wars without losing your shirt is a trick that most people would love to know. The cost of undisciplined discounting is phenomenal. My company recently conducted a study for a commercial real estate firm on the feasibility of RM principles in its business. To limit unbridled discounting, the company had placed strict controls on how much discounting was authorized at each sales staff level. The typical first-line salesperson, for instance, could grant a discount only up to 10% without higher approval. We found that the average discount given by first-line sales staff was 9.9%. Meanwhile, supervisors could grant up to a 20% discount without a manager's approval. Guess what? The average discount given by supervisors was 19.5%. Despite the appearance of a disciplined discounting policy, the company was routinely granting much deeper discounts than it intended to. Each sales level was giving away all it could.

It's especially interesting to watch companies in newly deregulated industries, like telecommunications, deal with this problem of discounting to meet competition. These companies have little experience with price wars, and the effects can be devastating. In recent years, AT&T, MCI, and Sprint have engaged in intense price-slashing strategies as each one tries to out-do the others in giveaway programs. The result? Losses of billions of dollars and thousands of jobs. Three other things have happened: consumers have had a field day running from competitor to competitor to get the lowest price; the consumer has perceived a lower value of the product, particularly in the case of discretionary purchases; and the bloodied companies have jacked up the full-rate prices for their highest-paying customers (usually business customers) to make up for the money they lost in the price war. Once companies engage in such price wars, it's a tough, uphill battle to convince the consumer that the product is worth the previous higher price. Additionally, those already paying the full bill aren't thrilled about taking a price hike to cover losses from the supplier's uncontrolled discounting practices. Revenue Management can help these companies limit their exposure in price wars by accurately assessing the impact of the competitors' actions in terms of consumer behavior and guiding them to respond in a way that meets the competition yet maximizes revenue.

Still, discounting and aggressive price actions will remain a fact of life in unregulated industries where competition is increasing. The discounting may take different forms, such as offering coupons or bundling "free" extras, but a discount is a discount, and companies must learn how to manage discounting in a way that maximizes revenue. The real issues here are *how much* to discount, *how many* discounts there should be, and *how much inventory* should be sold at *what price*. With all these issues, advanced RM concepts can help you understand customer behavior and optimize your response to the marketplace.

Even airlines, which are currently the most advanced in their use of RM, still make major mistakes. This is especially true when emotion overtakes reason in the decision-making process. In April 1992, for instance, American Airlines announced a new pricing structure called the "Value Plan." The plan simplified fares and reduced the gap between the highest and lowest fares, which had become extreme as years of pricing actions had made full fares higher and discount fares lower. Theoretically, the Value Plan would prompt deep-discount customers to trade up to slightly higher fares to take advantage of flexible, unrestricted tickets.

In a matter of a few weeks, however, the plan backfired, when Northwest launched a "Parents Fly Free" program, touching off what is commonly referred to as the "Airline Bloodbath of 1992." To protect market share, most airlines threw all their summer seat inventory into successive rounds of deeper discounting. They carried 470 million passengers on the cheap fares and broke passenger records, but lost $2 billion in the process.

One airline, however, forced itself to focus on revenue maximization instead of market share and concentrated on reducing its exposure to the frenzied discounting. Continental Airlines reasoned that if its competitors were selling all their summer seats at the cheapest fares during the fare war, they would have few, if any, seats available for later-booking, higher-fare passengers. Instead of selling all its seats at the fare-war rates, Continental held back a significant number of seats for later-booking passengers and later sold them at higher prices. Continental proved that if a company can keep its head, it does not have to be entirely at the mercy of its dumbest competitors.

RM TACTICS

To minimize your exposure to competitive discounting, you can employ these RM tactics very effectively:

- Use market-based pricing.
- Use segment pricing.

RAPIDLY CHANGING CIRCUMSTANCES

The last variable that RM techniques are adept at handling is the uncertainty caused by rapidly changing circumstances. Be-

cause of its dynamic nature, RM constantly reviews and re-
vises tactics in new situations. This is why broadcasters,
whose markets are being rapidly eroded by cable companies
and other forms of entertainment, are seeing success with
RM. Peter Kretz, general manager of the Canadian Broadcasting Corporation, was one of the first in the broadcasting industry to adopt these techniques. Other industries that are on
the brink of tremendous change and sudden increases in competition include electric and gas utilities, cable TV providers,
and local telephone markets.

Take the Internet, which is experiencing a period of astonishingly rapid change. The application of RM techniques
could be extremely helpful to firms eager to make money from
the explosion of opportunities presented on the Net. An example: Internet service provider Netcom reported that the
number of "hits" it has seen on its system grew from six million a day in August 1995 to forty million a day only six
months later. If Netcom could identify how its market is segmented and determine the behavioral characteristics of each
segment, it could explore differential pricing to maximize revenues. The broader access to the Net also presents revenue
opportunities in the sponsorship of certain "cybersites." In
1995, Microsoft paid $225,000 to sponsor the NFL/NBC
Sports Super Bowl Web site for six weeks. NBC is asking
$350,000 for a six-month sponsorship for its charter commer-
cial Web site.

The value of the pages will change rapidly as more, higher-
quality sites are available in cyberspace and more users access
them. But like any other product, sponsorship of these sites
will be a function of supply and demand. When Procter &
Gamble began advertising on the Internet in April 1996, the
cyberworld was excited, but P&G changed the rules of advertising in the deal. Instead of compensating the on-line compa-

nies for each consumer who sees a P&G ad, P&G will pay only when the on-line customer clicks from that ad to P&G's own Web sites. Now, only 1%–2% of the Web ads entice surfers to click on the advertisers' home pages. Advertising experts believe that the real advertising potential of the Web lies in sites that target users more narrowly. Even P&G backed down on its pricing demands when it signed with iVillage's "Parent Soup," which is directed to parents, a major P&G target group. It's obvious that commercial use of the Internet will be subject to even greater entropy and fragmentation than traditional media because of the incredibly fluid nature of the Internet.

Sometimes business indecision is caused by extraordinary events that create a lingering cloud of uncertainty. The major league baseball strike of 1994 is a case in point. Major league teams discovered that, after the strike was over, the fans did not return in 1995. Attendance was down an average of 20% below prestrike levels. Revenue from broadcasting and cable dropped proportionately. A number of teams lost in excess of $20 million. The Houston Astros gave away tickets, and the Florida Marlins were selling seats as low as $1 in September. These were desperate responses to an uncertain marketplace. The application of sophisticated RM techniques could have helped the teams understand the changes in perceived value and kept price discounting to a minimum.

RM TACTICS

Dealing with rapidly changing circumstances is a major challenge. But using these RM tactics will help ensure that your company responds in a knowledgeable, and revenue-optimal, way:

- Forecast at the micromarket level.
- Maximize revenue through optimal timing.
- Arm the soldiers fighting the micromarket wars.

We all know that companies strive to understand where the market is headed, but maybe they go about this in the wrong way. Asked what made him such an outstanding player, hockey great Wayne Gretsky responded, "All the other guys go where the puck *is;* I head to where it's *going to be.*" But how do you predict where the puck is going to be in business? Sometimes, elementary powers of observation lead you in the right direction. Smart companies, whether small or large, are good not only at forecasting revenues but also at forecasting opportunities. The bigger a company is, however, the more it needs sophisticated RM tools for the forecasting process, because making creditable predictions in today's highly charged and fast-moving competitive environment often takes a huge amount of data crunching. When the marketplace is changing rapidly, companies need to respond rapidly, which means developing the ability to analyze change with the speed of change itself.

LAUNCHING THE REVENUE ROCKET

My experience is that, outside of the airline or hotel business, they like the concept of Revenue Management, but they have no idea how to effectuate it.

—HERB KELLEHER, CHAIRMAN AND CEO,
SOUTHWEST AIRLINES, INC.

EVALUATING THE RM POTENTIAL

B Y NOW IT SHOULD BE clear that Revenue Management can apply to virtually all businesses. Applications range from simply adopting the RM attitude and thinking about supply, demand, and pricing management in RM terms, to using high-powered algorithmic tools. What level of Revenue Management is reasonable and appropriate for you? The answer depends on the market environment, the size of your company, and the marketing tactics used by you and your competitors.

The power of the RM attitude is in focusing your company on revenue and then using the basic techniques of RM to convert market uncertainty to probability and probability to revenue gain. Many companies can achieve significant revenue gains merely by adopting a revenue-driven attitude and applying the core concepts of Revenue Management. The key is understanding your micromarkets, figuring out how to segment them, and determining the price sensitivity of each segment to your product's attributes. That's what Carol Meinke did in her one-chair barbershop. She segmented the customers into two groups, convenience-oriented customers and price-oriented customers, and was able to create two new programs that addressed the needs of each. In satisfying those needs, she generated more revenue from each market segment.

Carol didn't need a high-tech approach to RM, but companies with millions of customer transactions annually will never achieve their optimum revenue potential without computer assistance. Too much data and too many variables make it impossible for humans to respond to the market in a timely and practical way. In these cases, computers speed the process, do the data-crunching work faster and more accurately than people, and provide the information needed for the decisions that only people can make.

During the last dozen years, my associates and I have developed three diagnostic tests designed to determine a company's real revenue-generating factors (which are often very different from the apparent factors), analyze how much untapped revenue is available, and discover how it can be retrieved on a continuing basis. Our tests begin with a look at the seven uncertainties in a company's market. The extent to which the company encounters several or all of these variables, as well as the degree of uncertainty it faces in each, forms the basis for the RM tools and process recommendations. These recommendations focus on a company's individual revenue opportunity and what will work for it. Of course, no two companies are exactly alike in processes, structure, leadership, and politics, all of which affect revenue-generating activities. Still, these diagnostics can be adapted to apply to virtually any company seeking to maximize its revenues.

The three tests are as follows:

- **Foundation Survey:** This test is for groundbreaking companies in industries where Revenue Management has not yet been widely adopted. It defines the characteristics of the industry, evaluates the company and its market, and examines how RM could be applied. We also provide a high-level estimate of the benefits (including the potential revenue gain in actual dollars) of applying RM.
- **Needs Evaluation:** With this step, we begin to define a company's relevant micromarkets. We use simulation software to determine the best ways to forecast micromarket behavior and optimize price and availability given the company's capacity, costs, and competitive constraints. This gives us an accurate picture of the revenue potential and determines the best way to achieve it. We then recommend the systems, processes, and organization that will maximize revenue; we also spell out the cost of the investment, quantify the benefits (which include actual revenue return figures), and provide a detailed RM project plan that specifies delivery dates, tasks, responsibilities, and time lines.
- **Revenue Audit™:** This diagnostic test evaluates an existing RM program to determine whether a company is achieving its revenue potential from RM. Using a set of interviews and data diagnostic techniques, we can determine actual revenue benefits derived from current RM practices, how much more revenue opportunity is still available, where it is, and how to get it. Processes,

organization, and market issues are examined; we also use computer simulations to analyze current pricing, sales, inventory, and RM actions. In my view, auditing the revenue side of the income statement should be considered as important to the company as its current financial audit.

These tests (all proprietary) are available to any company that hires my firm. But my intention here is to show you how you can diagnose your company's RM potential on your own.

THE PATH TO REVENUE MANAGEMENT

Let's say you've decided that the principles of Revenue Management apply to your market, you know that you've got untapped revenue opportunity, and you're champing at the bit to go get it. You've been burned by the company's attempts at reengineering and total quality management. Now what? How do you implement RM to achieve a successful result?

First, understand that total quality management and reengineering are essentially management *arts* subject to the interpretation of whoever is in charge of these programs. There is no established process that can be applied to every business to achieve the goals of these management concepts, which is why so many of these programs have been minimally effective or have failed outright, costing companies a lot of time and money in the process.

In its most sophisticated form, Revenue Management is a *science*. By definition, it establishes and organizes facts, principles, and methods and then measures performance. As with any major undertaking, you must know where you are going, how to get there, and how to know whether you've arrived. It sounds simple, but the hardest part is thinking through the process, establishing objectives, and creating a plan that will work in your environment.

When General Norman Schwarzkopf defined the secret of success behind the Gulf War's military operation as "having a clearly defined objective, and knowing how to accomplish it," he was describing a triumph of planning and information technology. Schwarzkopf's meticulously planned strategy resulted from fighting and refighting the war in sophisticated computer simulations; potential tactics were tested thousands of times with "virtual" troops long before the real troops invaded Kuwait. Once the invasion began, every action was guided by real-time computer tracking, and real-time adjustments were made as indicated. Similarly, a company must set clear and manageable objectives, communicate these objectives to everyone in the organization, and insist on an unwavering focus of people and resources on the mission. RM can be tremendously helpful in achieving that focus.

NINE STEPS TO SUCCESS

Success depends on the effective adaptation of its techniques to your particular markets, products, competition, culture, corporate mission, and constraints. Though there's no single "RM way," there is a process that can be followed to establish a successful RM program in any environment. This process consists of nine steps:

1. Evaluate your market needs.
2. Evaluate your organization and processes.
3. Quantify the benefits.
4. Enlist technology.

5. Implement forecasting.
6. Apply optimization.
7. Create teams.
8. Execute, execute, execute.
9. Evaluate success.

STEP #1: EVALUATE YOUR MARKET NEEDS.

The essential first step is evaluating your market needs and defining the necessary elements of an appropriate RM project in considerable detail. Sometimes, the needs evaluation is difficult to complete because once employees (especially senior managers) learn about RM and its revenue-generating power, they can become extremely impatient. They want to go after the revenue right away. They don't want to be slowed down by what appears to be an unnecessary exercise. They want to "just do it." They would rather skip the most important and by far the hardest part: *thinking through the project!*

Not long ago, I made a presentation on RM to the senior staff of a large Asian airline. I had been there a couple of times before, and they had worked through some tough cultural issues and were beginning to see the value of RM for their airline. I ended my presentation by explaining the first step, the needs evaluation. The senior vice president of marketing was an early advocate of Revenue Management in the company and was ready to move right away on the project. But he didn't want any part of this needs evaluation. He wasn't buying my argument that, if done properly, the needs evaluation would actually speed up the delivery of a successful RM program. It had taken him a long time to convince the others that the airline was losing money without sophisticated RM, and now that he had gotten their attention he was impatient to get a computer system installed. "We just need a system," he said. "We don't want you to come in here and tell us what our needs are. We've been looking at this for two years. *We know our needs.*"

I paused, unsure of how to proceed. "Just exactly what are your needs?" I asked.

"We are giving too many discount seats to low-yield groups," he replied.

"That's not the biggest issue," said another vice president in the meeting. "We're getting killed by new competition on the transpacific route."

"No," said another, "we have a horrible no-show problem on the domestic routes and it's costing us millions."

Another piped in with a different issue. Then another. I let them argue back and forth about their needs for fifteen minutes. Finally, I said, "Thank you all for validating the requirement for a needs evaluation far more eloquently than I could." We started the needs evaluation the next week.

STEP #2: EVALUATE YOUR ORGANIZATION AND PROCESSES.

When my firm performs a needs evaluation, the principle objective is to define and document specific issues that a company must address to maximize revenues. The process involves an intensive review of the organization, practices, policies, and procedures that are involved in revenue production. An enormous amount of information is gathered in a three-stage effort of interviews, documentation, and data gathering, which is subjected to intense scrutiny.

Opportunities for revenue growth begin to surface as we gather comments and job descriptions from the CEO and the staff on all levels of sales, marketing, finance, operations, information technology, and other relevant departments. People are generally very cooperative and excited about being a part of the needs evaluation process; it's apparent to everyone that the contribution and attitudes of each individual in the company can greatly affect future profits. The interview process also begins to build a consensus as employees are forced to start thinking about the bigger picture. During this phase, many queries are versions of a single, basic question: "What drives our revenues?" Sometimes the answers are very enlightening and cause the company to rethink its position in the marketplace.

A few years back, my firm was engaged by a broadcasting company to determine whether RM could apply to its business. Since the broadcasting business was new to us, my colleagues and I began by developing an understanding of the issues that drive broadcasting revenues. At the end of the first week of interviews, we gathered the senior managers together to ask a key question.

"Exactly what is it that you sell?" I asked.

"Advertising spots, of course," one person replied somewhat disdainfully. "Each hour, we have twelve thirty-second spots we have to sell."

Another person corrected him. "No, we sell eyeballs and earlobes. We sell exposure to an audience."

A third person saw it differently. "The advertisers don't just want exposure to eyeballs and earlobes, they want to get the message to a particular target audience, such as men twenty-five to forty-five years old in a certain income bracket."

Now we were at the nub of the problem. What they were selling (commercial spots) and what the customers were buying (exposure of their message to a specific demographic group) were two different things!

The first issue in Revenue Management is to understand what the customer is buying as opposed to what you are offering. A sandwich shop owner thinks he is selling sandwiches, but his customers think they are buying sustenance. They have choices about where they can get it: from home, a salad bar, a chicken place, or a pizza parlor. This big-picture understanding is essential before you can begin addressing the marketplace intelligently. It is also the starting point for understanding the micromarkets. If you don't understand what you are selling in relation to what your customers are buying, you open yourself up to stealth competitors—those from unexpected quarters who sneak in to steal your customers, like the low-cost airlines who drained customers away from Greyhound Bus Lines.

Documentation of how your company operates will often uncover issues that have been inhibiting revenue maximization. You should look carefully at organization charts, job descriptions, internal directives, and even policies and procedures manuals. You'll discover that one department's objectives may conflict with those of the company as a whole. For instance, paying sales staff a commission purely on volume alone, irrespective of the profitability of the transaction, can be in direct conflict with corporate profitability targets.

Gathering accurate and complete data is the most difficult part of a needs evaluation process, but it is also one of the most important. Data is the driving force behind the quantitative analysis, which helps determine the value of the revenue opportunities being missed and can be captured by RM. The data you need to analyze includes virtually anything that reflects the products offered, the prices, competition, and customer behavior.

Unfortunately, many companies routinely discard historical sales data. Information about customer behavior is a valuable corporate asset that can reveal consumer behavioral patterns, the impact of competitors' actions, and other important market information. You must keep complete records of every transaction your company makes—without them, the journey to RM wisdom cannot be initiated.

STEP #3: QUANTIFY THE BENEFITS.

Quantifying the benefits of Revenue Management *before* starting the project is a critically important step when embarking on the RM project. Setting revenue targets is essential. You should know how much revenue you can obtain from Revenue Management, where it is, and how to go about getting it. It's reckless to start with the attitude that "there's a lot of dough out there, so let's just start up an RM program and go get it." The quantification step is important, but it doesn't necessarily have to be complex or time consuming. It depends on the nature of the business, the amount of information available, and the effort required to justify the next steps. The most important thing about the quantification step is that it results in a revenue target that everyone believes in and that can be achieved. Further, the target can justify the resources a company will deploy to pursue the new opportunity for revenue.

For many businesses just getting into Revenue Management, making a few reasonable assumptions is sufficient to create this target. Our original RM program at Delta Air Lines was based on the simple assumption that if Delta could convert just one discount passenger to full fare on each flight, it would be worth $52 million annually. If you run a small business and want to adopt a no-tech approach to RM, you can do the same. For example, a golf course manager might calculate that if he raised his greens fees 20% for peak weekend tee times, he could lose 10% of his business and still make an additional $200,000 per year.

But for many businesses, simple assumptions are not enough; because of the complexity of their markets and products, they require a much more sophisticated analysis. If you manage a large business, you should strive to use as much information technology as you can, but it must address your individual situation, not someone else's. For large companies particularly, simulation modeling can help assess the marketplace, quantify the revenue benefits, and choose the best course of action.

With simulation modeling you perform various experiments in a computerized representation of the real environment. It is most effective in evaluating approaches to problems when experimentation in the "live" environment is impractical or impossible. In corporate decision making, true simulation modeling is a relatively new concept. However, simulations can be useful in understanding a business environment and learning how to adapt to it. Simulations are frequently used to "prefly" space shuttle missions, train pilots, test the crash worthiness of aircraft and automobiles, and evaluate battlefield strategy. Similarly, businesses are increasingly finding that simulation is an indispensable tool for evaluating and testing millions of alternatives.

My colleague Dick Niggley has a background in developing war games for the War College of the U.S. Department of Defense. He has successfully adapted war simulation modeling concepts to assess the impact of various marketing strategies and tactics. To accurately reflect the "live" marketing environment, these models require enormous amounts of consumer behavior data. It isn't unusual to use more than 1 gigabyte of data in a marketing simulation analysis. This process goes far beyond the average spreadsheet "what if" analysis; in fact, for companies that understand it, it's usually the most comprehensive analysis they have ever done.

Simulation software is now more widely available for commercial use. Simulation models analyze your company's historical transaction data to reveal the revenue opportunities, the amount of revenue that can be achieved, the source of the revenue, and the reason your company is failing to capture it. They often uncover practices you thought were productive but actually were preventing you from achieving your full revenue potential. The modeling process should also be used to set new revenue targets for your company, which will make it possible to cost out the benefits of going after the revenue opportunity. For instance, if the simulation exercise shows that you can achieve a $500,000 annual benefit, the level of RM effort should be evaluated against this expected outcome. Potential annual revenue gains of $5 million or $50 million would justify greater levels of RM effort. The new revenue targets also serve as a rallying point to keep everyone at your company focused on these revenue objectives and the RM project on course.

The needs evaluation process results in a clearly defined set of objectives based on achievable revenue gains. It also defines the conceptual design of computer systems, sets organizational requirements and time frames, and recommends policy and procedural changes to enable your company to attain the identified revenue potential. It results in a detailed implementation plan with revenue targets, objectives, dates, deliverables, roles, and responsibilities. Typical objectives include the following:

- Improving market share in specific price-sensitive markets
- Employing opportunistic pricing in certain situations
- Reserving particular products for high-value customers and accounts
- Implementing new marketing programs
- Shifting bulk sales to periods of low demand

Finally, the needs evaluation assesses the inherent risks of the program. Throughout the study, you need to identify possible constraints and obstacles to implementing an effective RM program, as well as design steps that will ensure that these potential constraints do not impede the progress of the project or the program's ultimate effectiveness. Typical constraints include the following:

- Readiness of personnel to shift to a new philosophy
- Organizational inhibitors
- Data processing capabilities (hardware and software)
- Senior management's commitment to change
- Sales force objectives
- Capital requirements
- Communication to entire company

• Possible market resistance
• Buy-in from distribution outlets

The most successful Revenue Management programs are implemented by companies that take the time to assess and document their needs, clearly define their new revenue targets, and share the RM vision with everyone in the company. The implementation plans should include specific targets (even relatively modest ones) that are achievable within six months of the initiation of the program. Multimillion-dollar efforts with no payback for years (like those that have occurred in reengineering, total quality management, and other programs) sap vital energy and enthusiasm from the project. Regular victories in periodic, six-month intervals keep the project on track, demonstrate success to all involved, and generate cash to fund future efforts.

STEP #4: ENLIST TECHNOLOGY.

Most businesses could use technology better to understand their markets and improve the pricing and availability of their products in relation to market demand. Even without sophisticated analytical tools, tracking customer data and product usage over time can provide insights. For example, the proprietor of a one-chair barbershop will have between three hundred and four hundred regular customers and a variety of "products," such as haircuts, hair styling, perms, and hair coloring. Each might have a different price and a different cost in terms of time and materials. There will also be opportunity costs based on demand. A two-hour perm with a $10 margin displacing four haircuts with $5 margins results in a $10 opportunity cost.

If you manage a large company however, complex computational processes are required to perform high-level RM techniques, but RM should not just automate what is already being done manually. It should enable you to operate much more efficiently and profitably, because it provides you with information and market intelligence that you don't currently have. *RM is a business and economic science that should change the way you view your business and manage the core issues of product, supply, demand, and pricing.*

A systematic, effective approach must be taken in designing and building powerful RM tools. Failure to thoroughly understand the business requirements when building complex new software can lead to horrible consequences. In the early 1980s, for instance, the Burroughs Corporation embarked upon a project to build new central reservations and property management systems for the hotel industry, but after a lot of money had been expended, the project was floundering. Larry Hall, now a colleague of mine, joined Burroughs as a development manager and soon discovered why the project was adrift. "One Saturday, I went into the office and came across a programmer sitting at his computer terminal, banging away writing programs," Hall remembers. "I asked him what he was doing and he told me he was writing the check-in routine for the property management system. I asked him how he knew how the check-in routine should work, and he said he had stayed in a Holiday Inn once. He was going from his personal experience directly to hard computer code, with nothing else in between."

Astonishingly, nobody had identified the key issues and written a comprehensive project plan. The system was just bits and pieces built by programmers who came up with their own ideas about how it should be done and programmed accordingly. At that point in time, Burroughs had already invested about $7 million into the project, but everything had been done on the fly. If a programmer wanted to figure how to handle accounts receivable at a hotel property, he'd call up a friend for advice and then blow it into the code. There was no thought about marketing issues or product definition. Finally, the project was called to a halt while basic specifications were developed and defined.

"This was classic project mismanagement," relates Hall. "It was mind-boggling to me that there was so much energy put into a technology project with zero definition. The irony of this experience was that Burroughs was extraordinarily visionary for the time. The integrated architecture they were thinking about in the early eighties is exactly what hotel companies are trying to achieve today, fifteen years later." Unfortunately, the idea of integration at Burroughs died. It was just too expensive to continue pursuing it at the time.

Like any major system effort, Revenue Management system development must be a disciplined process. For the system to be effective, you must determine the requirements, design functionality, detail project planning, insist on constant user interaction, and establish accountability. These steps ensure that the end product fits your business requirements and is on time and on budget.

As should be clear by now, Revenue Management is a *core process* for companies. If you want to use RM to rake in those millions of dollars of incremental revenue and help you dominate the market at the same time, you need to begin by taking the time to thoroughly review all the issues relevant to revenue generation and then determine the best RM processes and tools for your company. If you are a senior manager, that means asking a lot of questions of the people charged with implementing RM. If you are presenting RM to senior managers, cover all the bases before you make your sales pitch up the ladder. When senior managers find out how much missed revenue the company is leaving on the table, they will want it right away. You want to be sure you can tell them just exactly what getting it will take.

STEP #5: IMPLEMENT FORECASTING.

Forecasting and optimization are the functions of a Revenue Management system that set it apart from any other corporate computer applications. They are the engines of the marketing machine. Without the forecasting and optimization components, the RM system would still be valuable as a huge data warehouse. However, the real value of the data is in using it to predict customer behavior and deciding what actions to take to maximize revenue. This is what advanced forecasting and optimization at the micromarket levels permits.

Forecasting nonconformist consumer behavior in an amoeba market is tricky. Ideally, you should establish a forecasting model that uses as much as 100% of the company's past transactions for at least the previous twelve months. In addition, you should incorporate seasonality and historical trends into the forecast to account for cyclical patterns. Finally, you should adjust the forecast to account for iatrogenic effects—actions (or inactions) by the company that may have influenced the historical booking patterns. For example, if your company sold out of product, there might have been demand beyond what the sales figures show. The demand must be "unconstrained" to account for what the market would have purchased if you had an adequate supply of product. Only then can an accurate picture of the future be obtained.

Forecasting is easy, but getting good forecasts is difficult. One hotel company hired a college professor to develop a forecasting model. His theory was to take all the data he could possibly get, dump it into a mathematical model, and let the model sort out variables that might have predictive value. Theoretically, that could have worked over time, but there was a lot of "noise" in the preexisting data and the variables changed too rapidly. The result was that the professor could not come up with a useful forecast. His model always lagged the market by months.

In today's amoeba market, increasing numbers of data observations are required on a more frequent basis to accurately predict the future.

THE THREE RULES OF GOOD FORECASTING

- The forecasts must be at the right level of detail.
- An appropriate amount of data must be analyzed.
- Frequent reforecasting must occur.

Revenue maximization requires segmenting customers into the narrowest possible categories to understand their characteristics, including purchase patterns, perception of the product, and willingness to pay. Discernible micromarkets should be separately forecast, which for most large companies means digesting a phenomenal amount of data to get accurate results. The forecasting system my company built for Hilton Hotels, for example, contains 200 gigabytes of data. If this data were converted to printed pages and stored in Hilton's corporate library, it would consist of 133,000 volumes, take up 3.2 miles of shelf space, and weigh 166 tons!

Over the years, my company has built dozens of large forecasting systems for clients, and I can say with a high degree of confidence that there are three secrets to accurately forecasting the behavior of nonconformist consumers in the amoeba market: *reforecast, reforecast, reforecast.* Things happen every day that destroy the accuracy of your forecast, no matter how much data you use or how accurate your forecasting methodology is. The only way to keep up with the increasingly entropic market is through reviewing, reassessing, and reforecasting.

For most of our clients, RM computer systems review every day's sales activity, the consumer response to changes in product or price, and other relevant accessible data. Computer forecasts are run overnight to give decision makers fresh knowledge about the market and consumer behavior the first thing each morning. Clients who experience tremendous market activity during the course of a day may require reforecasting hourly, or even more frequently. Often, we consider the possibility of reforecasting after every customer transaction. Studies indicate that the improvements in decision making from such a reforecast *can increase a company's revenues 1%–2%.* For a billion-dollar company, this represents $10–20 million annually.

STEP #6: APPLY OPTIMIZATION.

Forecasting suggests what customers are likely to do. Optimization suggests what you should do about it. Optimization algorithms are mathematical routines that will either maximize or minimize a given function. In space shots, flight paths between bodies are minimized, and so is fuel burn. For commercial enterprises, we want to minimize costs and maximize revenues. Optimization algorithms have been developed for maximizing revenues through pricing and inventory control in a number of industries. This is a great practical use of rocket science.

"Think of optimization as the computer game of Tetris," says Kevin Geraghty, a colleague of mine. "The variety of customers with different needs and different values are like the falling blocks that have different shapes. Your productive capacity is the space to be filled with the blocks. You want to fit the different-sized and -shaped blocks perfectly together so that every space is filled. You turn the blocks to fit into the gaps. If you leave a gap, that's the same as unused capacity. Once an empty space is covered by the next level because no blocks coming down fit or you didn't move fast enough to position a descending block into the gap, you can't go back and fill it in later. You've lost that opportunity forever."

The same is true with business opportunity. If an airport hotel sells its last available room for a one-night stay on Wednesday, it won't be available for someone who might want it for a week. Optimization is about evaluating multiple options on how to sell your product and to whom to sell your product. It requires forecasting all the future demand and capacity possibilities and making the choices that will lead to the greatest revenue.

Typically, we find that Revenue Management programs produce 3%–7% in additional revenue. But the cost of generating this new revenue is usually minimal; indeed, for most companies, 80% of the new revenue goes directly to the bottom line. That's what we mean by driving the bottom line by growing the top line.

STEP #7: CREATE TEAMS.

As with any human endeavor, people will ultimately be the key to the success of Revenue Management in the company. RM projects are high profile because they represent a significant revenue gain for the company. Generally, everyone in the company is interested in the impact of a Revenue Management program on marketing, on current information technology resources, and on the way diverse groups coordinate their activities.

Senior management leadership and support are essential. Revenue maximization should be at the top of every CEO's list. What could be more important to your company than profitable revenue growth? And because they set the tone for the organization, senior managers can also help overcome the natural resistance to change. They also must provide adequate resources to the RM program if the company is to reap the highest potential revenue from RM. Finally, they must ensure that the best and the brightest people are on the RM team.

One of the most important components of every RM project is a Revenue Management champion. This must be someone of stature and leadership in the organization who is a passionate believer in the objectives of Revenue Management.

Ideally, the champion is part of the project from the beginning, has full authority to drive the project, and is a team builder. The champion must develop a consensus among management on the direction of the RM program. Lone Rangers don't do well in this role. They tend to alienate others, whose commitment is essential to success.

In small companies, it may not be feasible to set up a separate Revenue Management department, but it is important that someone in the organization be responsible for Revenue Management functions on an ongoing basis. Some midsize companies establish a Revenue Management group within the marketing department. In larger companies, however, a Revenue Management department is recommended.

The Revenue Management department should have full control of the revenue, and the company should expect accurate measurement of revenue results from this group. Your RM department should be staffed with highly trained professionals who are compensated according to a results-based compensation package. Controlling the revenue means that the RM department has the responsibility for the revenue, is accountable for the revenue, and has complete authority over the revenue. Defining the scope of accountability, responsibility, and authority is especially important, not only for the department charged with controlling the revenue but for the rest of the company as well. In general, however, the RM department should be held accountable for revenue performance, should be solely responsible for overseeing the Revenue Management program, and should have the ultimate decision on price and product availability for any new business.

Once the Revenue Management program has been established, senior management should continue to be involved by establishing direction and new objectives, supplying ongoing resources and support, and measuring the performance of the group. However, because of the micromarket tactics of Revenue Management, the implementation team must have a high degree of autonomy. The team will have to be responsive to rapid market changes, and decisions must be made instantly at the lowest level possible. Along with the authority to make these decisions must go the responsibility for them.

Steve Swope, a colleague who has set up Revenue Management organizations in over twenty companies around the world, says that the most important requirement of an RM organization is that it reflect the individual company's unique market situation. There is no magic formula that fits all needs; however, there are some well-established principles, the most important being that the individual who is held accountable for revenue performance should be the individual who controls the revenue. This is not the case in a number of companies. Subtle and not so subtle changes in pricing, inventory management, and sales processes over the years tend to shift the control of the revenue away from those originally designated with this responsibility. Some companies have never even addressed the question of who should be charged with controlling the revenue.

Lack of continuity between accountability and authority to control revenue can totally undermine the Revenue Management program and its ability to maximize revenues for a company. For instance, in a needs evaluation for a $600 million company a few years ago, one of the first issues we wanted to understand was how the company positioned itself in the market vis-à-vis its competitors. In doing so, we sought to understand its pricing strategy. Did it see itself as a low-price leader? Or did it wish to establish itself as a premium product with superior value and price? Just what was its pricing strategy? No one could articulate it. It was neither in writing nor in the collective minds of the company's employees. Prices were set as an uncoordinated response to competitors' actions, irrespective of the company's own objectives.

In another situation, the sales department was calling the shots on discounted volume selling. It could independently negotiate the price at which the product would be sold to a particular customer set. Clearly, the sales department for the company was controlling the revenue. But because a sales representative relates solely to his or her particular accounts, he or she cannot possibly understand the impact the collection of similar transactions can have on the company's overall revenue. In this case, the impact was devastating because the sales compensation was based on units sold rather than on revenue or profit generation!

As these examples suggest, it's important to carefully review who controls the revenue. For example, in most airlines, the local city personnel are responsible primarily for the delivery of the product and customer satisfaction, not revenue. The head office is responsible for revenue generation. The hotel industry, however, is set up differently. In many major hotel chains, headquarters deals with brand management, quality control, and franchising, but the responsibility, accountability, and authority for revenue is squarely in the office of the general manager of each individual hotel property. The local property is totally responsible for its own profitability.

While RM concepts are essentially the same, the way processes are designed and applied can be significantly different in decentralized organizations. Implementing RM in a decentralized organization usually involves an RM support group at headquarters, which instructs, trains, updates, measures, and recommends Revenue Management programs at the local level. In some instances, the technology is centralized, while the use of it is decentralized.

Whatever form an RM program takes, it's the responsibility of management to ensure that the company's RM organization and skills sets meet the needs of the program. Ten years ago, for instance, most airline revenue controllers were former reservations clerks and analysts, mainly because these people were already trained in the cryptic commands required to access the computer reservations system, where the inventory controls then resided. RM was commonly viewed as a stand-alone discipline, as were pricing, scheduling, advertising, and sales. The connections among all these facets of marketing had not yet been forged. As it became clearer that RM formulated a product from pricing and schedules and then delivered that product to the market, the skills set of revenue controllers changed from former reservations agents and analysts to M.B.A.'s well versed in supply/demand economics. However, the airlines discovered that the M.B.A.-dominated RM department doesn't work optimally either, since M.B.A.'s tend to be upwardly mobile and their tenure as controllers is seldom longer than two or three years. For airlines—and for all companies large enough to dedicate an entire department to RM—the best RM departments have a balanced mix of experienced career inventory controllers (most of whom come from reservations, sales, or accounting) and M.B.A. short-termers, who bring new ideas into the department and then move on.

Ben Baldanza, senior vice president of pricing and route planning at Continental Airlines, has been involved in RM department rebuilding activities at a number of airlines. His overview of what it takes to establish a successful Revenue Management program is one of the best I've ever heard:

In creating a new RM department to replace an old structure, you have to destroy the old ways of thinking and doing business if they don't make sense in today's market. But you also have to accept the fact that if you're going to do a lot of new things, you're going to make some mistakes, and allow for that. You want to improve the RM system to get better data, and you want to use that data more efficiently across the company. You also want a structure where you have smart people, and give them the time to learn the tools, examine the data, and really understand the market. In the skill set for the revenue controllers of the 1990s, you need analytical ability, communications skills, problem-solving talent, decision-making ability, and acceptance of accountability. If you get people with these basic skills, you can teach them the airline business or whatever business you're in. A critical element is creating an effective management reporting and measurement structure. It's a fundamental truism of business today that if you can't *measure it,* you can't *manage it* effectively. It's essential that you know every day if you're managing this right.

Communications is also a big factor. You need to build links with other departments and with the field sales and operations people. One way to do this is organizing road shows to educate the company about Revenue Management and how it will help them. You want to have the field in the feedback loop. RM departments in the past have ignored the communications side and then found that nobody understood what they were doing. When people don't know what you're doing, you get blamed for a lot of things. Whether you're wrong or not, people suspect that you're doing it wrong. You need credibility in the company to be an effective Revenue Management organization. Tearing down and rebuilding the RM organization can be a painful process, but when the organization and leadership understands how to leverage the system, measure the results, and reward performance, the Revenue Management department becomes an exciting place to work.

STEP #8: EXECUTE, EXECUTE, EXECUTE.

The key to the success of any effort lies in its execution. Ideas are nothing. Implementation is everything. Any great strategy can be rendered useless by the way it is implemented. A good plan executed now is better than a great plan executed next year.

Revenue Management will touch on many aspects of your company. There will be resistance from people who have "never done it that way before." There will be anxiety created by the high expectations as the entire company refocuses on revenue. There will be salespeople who feel they are losing their authority. There will be risks, frustrations, and delays with huge computer projects.

The successful RM project endures all these, and more. The champion is the focal point for the project, and he or she must have the authority to plow through the delaying and disrupting issues and to make course corrections as the project evolves. Above all, the champion must be a positive influence and great motivator to keep things on track. Adherence to project plans is essential. If a milestone slips, the next slip is easier. Milestone meetings should celebrate the completion of each milestone, not just point out slips.

The search for incremental revenue should be fun. Consider setting up contests between groups of revenue controllers to generate the greatest amount of incremental revenue; these will help keep revenue controllers sharp and focused on the objectives. I'm convinced that these motivational tools are at least as important as all the other efforts in the development of an RM strategy. A contest we conducted at one company continued over the course of a year, and the status of the controller groups was posted monthly. During that year, some people worked weekends to find more revenue improvements and called in from vacation to check on the status of their products. The winners received cruises, airline tickets, and resort vacations as well as the time off to enjoy them.

STEP #9: EVALUATE SUCCESS.

To be successful, RM programs must have clearly defined objectives, which must be achieved. Be sure every member of the RM project team has individual objectives and is measured on the completion of those objectives. The measurement points should be taken frequently, at least once a month. Measurement criteria should include the completion of milestones such as establishing the organization, adopting new business policies and processes, and meeting system project progress plans according to the original timetable. The main thing to evaluate in the introduction of an RM program is, of course, the generation of incremental revenue. You'd be amazed at the companies that have spent millions on Revenue Management systems but don't have a clue about whether they have generated a nickel!

Some companies have astounding Revenue Management success stories, while others have muddled through Revenue

Management efforts with little, if anything, to show for them. The difference is *always* that the successful companies have set realistic revenue targets and then measured progress against them. Although the creation of revenue targets may make some people uncomfortable and impose pressure to produce, targets are essential to success. If everyone knows the goal and knows that they will be measured on the attainment of that goal, they will almost always find a way to achieve it.

Relative to other information technology investments, the payoff from RM systems is among the greatest. RM systems can generate annual returns *in excess of 200%*. The average gross annual return on investment from all information technology systems is 81%, according to a study conducted by Erik Brynjolfsson of the Massachusetts Institute of Technology. Studies have shown that computer applications that result in sales increases or price improvements have a greater impact on a company's profitability than those that reduce costs. Generally speaking, a 5% reduction in sales expenses increases profits by 3%; a 5% increase in sales volume increases profits by 20%; and a 5% increase in selling price increases profits by 50%. Even so, most companies still give priority to computer systems development based on cost reductions, not revenue gain. (See chart on page 188.)

According to Peter Drucker, "Successful companies must reinvent themselves every ten years." When you embark on the path to Revenue Management, you are taking a new perspective about the way you conduct your business. You are making a significant change when you focus your entire company on revenue. This is why I have emphasized the importance of taking the time to thoroughly think out every element of the Revenue Management program. The degree of success you will achieve with Revenue Management depends on it.

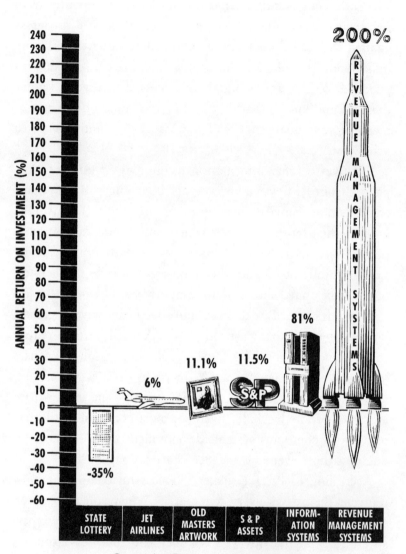

Comparing Returns on Investment

CHECKLIST: LAUNCHING THE REVENUE ROCKET

- **How Does RM Apply?** Examine the applicability of Revenue Management. How does the market exhibit the seven uncertainties addressed by RM?
- **How Much Is It Worth?** Use data analysis techniques to determine the untapped revenue potential.

  This involves three basic steps: (1) **Gather information**—Take a systematic approach to interviewing management and collecting data about revenue generation and control activities. (2) **Perform simulation analysis**—Analyze all available data to uncover hidden revenue potential through the computerized emulation of actual business environments and control processes. (3) **Assess costs versus benefits**—Detail revenue and other benefits versus the costs of different elements of RM.
- **How Do We Achieve the Highest Potential Benefits?** Establish a well-defined avenue for quantification of revenue benefits, organizational recommendations, computer system requirements, and procedural and policy recommendations for pricing, sales, inventory control management, and sales quotation processes.

CHAPTER

7

CASE STUDY: NATIONAL CAR RENTAL'S NEAR-DEATH EXPERIENCE

We decided to go for a revenue-based turnaround as opposed to a cost-cutting turnaround.
—LAWRENCE RAMAEKERS, TURNAROUND SPECIALIST
AND INTERIM PRESIDENT,
NATIONAL CAR RENTAL SYSTEM, INC.

ONE LAST CHANCE

IN MOST CASES, REVENUE Management is viewed as a means to generate additional revenues, but in some cases it can actually save a company from extinction. National Car Rental System is a case in point. By 1992, National had been losing money for at least a decade. That was fine when depreciation and tax write-offs were financial benefits for the owners or when National absorbed overproduction from its then parent, automaker General Motors. But the situation changed dramatically when GM announced a mind-boggling $3.4 billion loss for its 1991 fiscal year—the biggest corporate loss in history. It was clear that money-losing business units were a luxury that GM could no longer afford.

In December 1992, the future of the National Car Rental System unit was on the agenda at GM's board meeting. Twelve thousand jobs were on the line. There were two options: liquidate National Car or take a gigantic restructuring charge and give National one last chance to become profitable and then be sold at a price high enough for GM to recoup some of its investment. Given the urgency of GM's own situation, it was a tough decision. Liquidation would mean a $2 billion hit on its balance sheet. Restructuring to give National another chance meant that GM would have to take a whopping $744 million charge, and there was no guarantee that National would survive.

In the end, GM decided to give National one more chance to live. Just two years later, the decision paid off brilliantly. By early 1995, National had effected a $3 billion swing in value and was experiencing an *annual growth rate of about 20%*. It had gone from being a liability to being an attractive asset for acquisition. According to those directing this turnaround, *Revenue Management was the single most important factor*. Previously, National had been the fifth largest airport rental car company in the United States. Using RM, National achieved new power in the marketplace and was now in fourth place and rapidly closing in on the next largest contender.

The story of this achievement illustrates what can happen when a company turns its focus away from cost-cutting to revenue growth. It shows the power of Revenue Management when it is applied with the right combination of people, processes, systems, and determination. National Car Rental is a huge Revenue Management success story, but it is also a story of huge obstacles that had to be overcome. National's turnaround was accomplished in a highly competitive and volatile marketplace that did not yield revenue growth easily. Further, it was done while under extreme pressure from an owner that demanded immediate results.

A CHANGING COMPANY IN A CHANGING INDUSTRY

In the 1980s, the U.S. car rental business went through a metamorphosis rivaling those caused by airline and telecommunications deregulation. Before 1986, owners of car rental firms used them for large depreciation and investment tax write-offs. Profitability was not their first concern, and rental car companies typically did not make money from renting cars. They made money from manufacturers' rebates on cars they purchased, selling cars after depreciating them rapidly and convincing renters to buy expensive "options" such as collision insurance. The depreciation write-offs evaporated because of U.S. tax code changes in the mid-1980s. Major automakers bought car rental companies to keep production lines going by supplying rental car fleets when overseas competition cut into U.S. retail sales. But shortly thereafter, new-car sales began to improve, and the automakers needed cars coming off the production line for retail sales, so they changed the terms and jacked up the prices for the rental car fleets. Once again, the basic economics of the car rental industry changed because of circumstances beyond their control.

As they entered the 1990s, car rental companies were faced for the first time in years with the necessity of making money from their core business of renting cars. To make matters worse, these companies were caught in a vise between rising fleet acquisition costs and eroding revenues from fierce pricing competition.

My original involvement with National Car Rental occurred in 1986–1987, when my firm was called in to determine whether National would benefit from Revenue Management. The tax reform act had just been passed, and the attorneys general of several states were neutralizing rental car insurance sales tactics. Our study indicated that the car rental industry was a prime candidate for RM, and we put together a prototype system for National to prove that RM could provide significant incremental revenue. Just as we were completing the study, however, National underwent a leveraged buyout (LBO) and new management came in, led by Vincent Wasik, whose business credentials included stints in the car rental and cruise line industries.

Wasik had assembled a management group (mostly from Hertz) by offering them substantial stock options and convincing them that they would eventually make big money when National's stock value took off. The LBO involved the usual practice of saddling the company with enormous debt to finance the takeover. Of course, this translated into a severe cost-cutting program to pay off the debt. One of the costs that was cut was the RM project. RM was an unknown discipline to Wasik and his team, and they did not realize that they were effectively cutting off what could have been a major source of revenue to help pay off the LBO debt.

Vincent Wasik served as National's CEO from 1987 to February 1992. He was considered by many to be a brilliant marketing strategist. He had a clear vision of the high level of customer service that car rental companies should provide, and National's strong commitment to this vision was a saving grace during bad times. Wasik believed in building databases with reams of customer information; he also wanted to develop the first frequent-renter program in the industry. Further, he invented National's Emerald Aisle concept, whereby members could go to one aisle at a National airport location, pick out the car they wanted, and swipe their Emerald Aisle card at the exit. The Emerald Aisle concept was ahead of competition and was a big success in the premium business market.

Wasik was a vocal opponent of Revenue Management techniques, although it is doubtful that he fully understood them. He insisted on personally setting all of National's rental rates and refused to permit others to be involved in the process. He often came into the office on weekends to set pricing for every car and every corporate location, which was a huge task. For example, setting rates for just one city, like Atlanta, for a period of sixty days meant establishing twelve thousand new rates by the time each car, car class, and day of the week (midweek, weekend, daily rates, weekly rates, advance rates, etc.) was taken into consideration. National had about 170 corporate locations, so the job of this rate-setting exercise was enormous. Inevitably, many simplifying assumptions had to be made at the aggregate-market level.

It is unclear whether National made much money in the previous decade, but it is certain that in the post-LBO period things started going downhill fast. To protect its investment in the cars it supplied to National's fleet, General Motors stepped in and bought about 80% of National's shares, giving National some breathing room. Vince Wasik and his team were retained, but the directive was clear that National had to start showing financial improvements, and fast. This was 1991, and GM knew that the company as a whole would be swimming in a deep sea of red ink by the end of the year.

Wasik organized a top-level strategy meeting that came to be known throughout the company as "the infamous pizza meeting." The meeting was intense and lasted for hours as the group tried to hammer out strategies that would put National in the black. As the dinner hour approached, pizzas were brought in to keep the action going, but it wasn't going well. With all the recent changes in the rental car industry, competitive activity was heating up and price was becoming a major factor. Yet all suggestions that National should advertise price or review pricing strategies were severely discouraged by Wasik. "National will never advertise another price," Wasik was quoted as saying. Someone brought up the issue of Revenue Management and suggested that the RM project be revived and that National review its pricing strategies since nothing else seemed to be working. This suggestion reportedly enraged Wasik, who declared that the next person who mentioned the subject of pricing or Revenue Management would be fired. He made it clear that he and only he would set the rates.

A few months after the pizza meeting, in early 1992, Wasik was bought out by GM and left. National was still skidding, but now, with Wasik out of the picture, the company could at least explore new ways of pricing. National also decided to have another look at Revenue Management techniques.

As a first step, National sent representatives to a Revenue Management conference in Dallas where they learned about my firm's advancing work in RM. In mid-1992, a team from National came to our offices in Atlanta for an exploratory meeting. This group became excited at the potential RM could create at National and called us back the next day to arrange for National's senior management team to visit our offices for a high-level review of RM concepts and processes. By that time, GM had appointed Tom Murphy, a top GM finance executive, to replace Vincent Wasik as CEO. Bob McKenna, who had come to National with the group from Hertz and was a highly respected and experienced rental car industry executive, remained as president. Ernest Johnson, a National executive, was charged with spearheading Revenue Management.

Even though the need for action was urgent—National was still losing about $1 million per month—the officers knew that they had only one last chance for survival. In addition to talking to us, they met with virtually everyone else who claimed some expertise in RM. Ernest Johnson carefully evaluated all the proposals. "When you talk about how to choose a system, all these people pop up from nowhere," he observed. Some offered the usual fuzzy recommendations, like "establish a lucid rates program and a well-thought-out incentive program." Others were essentially selling sales models that calculated bonuses for the sales force but were calling it Revenue Management. One suggested that the major factor was to "avoid creating political problems," and another used a thermometer to display forecast capacity from 0 to 100. The most dangerous proposal came from someone who claimed he had an RM computer system that he could install immediately and start making National money.

But Johnson knew what he wanted. "I wanted someone to help me understand what Revenue Management is and to help me understand where the opportunity is in *my* business. I wanted someone to help me understand where the pitfalls were in putting this into my company. I wanted someone to give me a map of what I had to do to build a system. I wanted a rough idea of the cost and a time line of what it was going to take to get there. I wanted someone to give me an idea what the organization should look like to get it done. I could never go to my senior management unless I had all these things. This is not something you pencil out on an afternoon on a napkin," says Johnson. "Without all those pieces, we couldn't have done it."

After National selected us as their RM partner, they asked

us what the next step would be, and we presented our proposal for a three-month needs evaluation. Some of National's management team didn't like the idea of a study; they merely wanted a computer system. We were equally insistent on a disciplined business process approach. We felt strongly that analyzing their needs was the right way to start the process of transforming National into a revenue-driven organization. It would have been foolhardy to just jump in and build a system. There are personnel, organizational, and process issues to address. With the stakes so high, we knew that we had to get it right the first time.

This comprehensive approach was most actively resisted by a couple of individuals who had jumped into developing their own RM system the minute Wasik had departed. Jack Livingston, the chief information officer, and Tom Bennett, the Electronic Data Systems (EDS) manager who was overseeing National's ten-year, $500 million information systems outsourcing agreement with EDS, were livid. They had been vocal advocates of RM, and almost before the door had shut behind Vince Wasik they had started to work on implementing it. They had established a group called the RAT (Rates Automation Team), whose purpose was to develop a RAM (Rates Automation Machine). Their theory was that they could monitor customer demand levels at each location with a central computer and send messages to the field locations to raise rates as the cars were being sold out.

Livingston and Bennett had expended a large number of man hours to develop some sort of inventory management program, but all they were able to come up with were four simple reports. They were generating tons of paper (they jokingly measured the size of the report in hectares of timberland), but the company saw little revenue gain. They were thinking in the right direction, but their approach relied on the field offices taking action only after a large percentage of the cars had already been sold.

With Bob McKenna's help, Livingston and Bennett eventually came around. But their resistance was a vivid reminder of how hard it can be to change a company in midstream. After all, both these men were sympathetic to what we were doing; when top-level people are suspicious of the entire concept, forward progress can be very slow. But if you appeal to a manager's desire to do what's best for the company, sometimes—as was the case with Livingston—those who at first resist will later become your biggest supporters and real believers in Revenue Management.

ENTER THE TURNAROUND CONSULTANTS

We started the needs evaluation on January 4, 1993, right after National had gotten the reprieve from its parent, General Motors. Shortly thereafter, we learned that GM had independently hired the turnaround firm of Jay Alix and Associates (JA&A) to come into National, spearhead the turnaround of the company, and get it ready for sale. We were concerned because JA&A had a reputation as a rabid costcutter. I was afraid it was déjà-vu all over again.

Jay Alix assumed the position of chairman of the board of National, and Larry Ramaekers was installed as president to run the day-to-day turnaround operation. Their modus operandi was to clean out the top executive group first, so many who had supported our project left National shortly after JA&A came in.

"Unfortunately, my most important decision is whom do I fire first," says Ramaekers. "I deal only with troubled companies. The problem is almost always the people who have made decisions that aren't working. If you come in and clean house of those people the employees believe caused the problem, then they get behind you fairly quickly."

Once Alix and Ramaekers moved the senior managers out of National, they began to concentrate on doing things that could provide quick success, such as reducing the time limits on receivables from sixty days to thirty days and installing tough cost control measures. Before long, however, Ramaekers realized that National's costs had already been cut to the bone and that there were few significant gains to be achieved by further cost-cutting. Ramaekers concluded that revenue generation was the only way National could make it and that Revenue Management was the key. "We became convinced that the company could succeed and decided that Revenue Management could provide a significant portion of the dollars we needed to turn the place around."

The needs evaluation was already under way by then, and it uncovered a number of practices that National had to reapproach; it also revealed tremendous revenue opportunity. For example, in case after case, a car would be sold for only one day during the week or just for a weekend. Later requests for an entire week's rental had to be turned down because there was no inventory available for those one or two days. Then the car would sit unrented on the lot for the other five or six days.

After Wasik left, National had decentralized pricing, and now each city was determining its own pricing strategy. The needs evaluation uncovered several different pricing strategies, including the following:

- **The Tail of the Dog:** Copy whatever everybody else is doing.
- **The Hertz-Minus:** If Hertz was the market leader, set

prices at $2 less than Hertz regardless of market conditions.

- **The Alamo-Plus:** Our product is better than Alamo's, so set the price to reflect a premium over Alamo.
- **The Middle of the Road:** Charge something in between Alamo and Budget.
- **The Ad Department Rate:** Offer a $16 weekend rate set by the advertising department unilaterally.

All these strategies were developed irrespective of demand and the positioning of National's fleet versus competitors (oversupply or undersupply). My perspective was that these weren't strategies at all but knee-jerk reactions to competitors' movements. Now, instead of the CEO controlling prices, National had its competitors controlling its prices!

WHAT IS REVENUE MANAGEMENT WORTH?

At the conclusion of our needs evaluation, we reported that National could earn *$58 million annually* from RM, which represented a 9% increase on its current revenue base of $750 million. This was the largest percentage increase we had ever related to a client, but we knew it was there. Of course, there were skeptics—the $58 million number was just too big for them to accept.

We reviewed the process we used to arrive at this number. We had thoroughly analyzed a huge chunk of National's own data—capturing all the company's business over the previous seven months. It included all transactions (bookings, cancellations, and rentals) at all 170 corporate locations. It was incredibly detailed, with each transaction analyzed by location, car class, and day of week. With this information in hand, we could show the company how much it actually made or lost as a result of an individual transaction or collection of transactions. And the data was all at the micromarket level. Even the skeptics were convinced by this array of powerful evidence; they, too, saw that we were on to something that could save the company.

Our first step was recommending a program that would revolutionize the way National approached pricing. We also described the organization structure required to support an effective RM program and what kind of people should be selected for the RM staff. We detailed the process of managing the revenue and talked about the relationship the RM department should have with the rest of the organization. Finally, we outlined the specifications for the high-powered RM system they needed. This would be state of the art for both RM and the car rental industry. That capability, if used with the right tactics, would give National one hell of a competitive edge.

We laid out a two-year plan to make the program fully functional. Along the way, however, many steps would generate significant incremental revenues. "Not fast enough," they said. In the pre-JA&A discussions, National management had indicated that the system would have to be "self-funding," but Ramaekers scotched that. "If this thing is as big as you're suggesting, then we want to get it done," he said. "It's critical to the turnaround of this company. Forget the self-funding. I'll get it funded." This was not a trivial matter. They were looking at a $10 million investment in a company that had been losing a million a month for years. But they insisted that we implement the program faster.

We revised our plan accordingly. Because of the urgency of National's situation (GM wanted a fast turnaround to sell the company as quickly as possible), we recommended an interim system with some basic elements that could be developed in a couple of months and provide National some level of revenue improvement while we worked on the big system. We called the interim step "Phase .5." We didn't want to call it "Phase 1" because we wanted everyone to recognize that this was just a half step. We were afraid that once the first step was accomplished National's management might revert to cost-cutting mode and kill the next step of the project, where the real revenue production would occur.

The Phase .5 system would produce forecasts and rate recommendations, distribute the rates to the in-house reservation system for sale, and provide several key reports. It would do this nightly for the top thirty-eight cities based on revenue impact. Because of the needs evaluation, we were able to focus on the 22% of locations that gave us 60% of the revenue potential. We indicated that we could have the Phase .5 system up and running in about four and a half months—that's how long it would take to write and test the software code, install the hardware, and assemble an RM department. This was an aggressive schedule. But Ramaekers thought it wasn't aggressive enough. We proposed to be finished by September; he wanted everything in place to take advantage of the July/August peak season—an almost impossible task. Our project director, Tim Hart, was aghast. Unrelenting, Ramaekers applied a lot of pressure, explaining, "When you're dealing with a sick company, prudent time periods are not acceptable. When you've got a company that's on life or death, you've got to make it go faster."

Making it go faster meant a superhuman effort on the part of the National/Aeronomics RM team. Not only did we have the system to deal with, there were several difficult issues that involved resources and elements that were new to National's data processing environments. We also had to design the RM components, develop the RM department, and train the revenue controllers—not to mention educate the local managers in the affected cities.

Phase .5, the quick and dirty "throwaway" system, involved two basic objectives: to establish a central point for inventory control to maintain accurate inventory availability, and to collect relevant data (reservations, availability, capacity, postarrival, rates, etc.) into an RM database that would build the future demand forecasts and manage the inventory and rates to maximize revenues.

The second phase of the project, Phase 1, was much more complicated. It required the development and implementation of a state-of-the-art Revenue Management system for the car rental industry. This system would be a Windows-based application and operate on a local area network (LAN). It would use client-server architecture allowing users to interpret and analyze data and to communicate rate and inventory changes instantaneously to intracompany systems and to the Airline Tariff Publishing Company. From there, they would be distributed to the global distribution systems, from which travel agents book cars. The demand forecasting piece would support length-of-rent optimization at the same time it forecast arrival date activity. The optimization function would address overbooking and apply minimum length-of-rent parameters in inventory recommendations. The system would also assist in fleet planning.

When we began implementation on May 1, 1993, we essentially had nothing. Not only did we have to design and build two systems, we had to work with National to effect a profound change in its business processes and cultural philosophies. There is nothing more difficult to change in people than ingrained beliefs and attitudes. Many people still believed that money could be made simply by cutting the fleet and raising the prices across the board; we had to convince them that the real money could be made only on the micromarket level by managing every single rental transaction separately.

THE REVENUE MANAGEMENT CHAMPION

Meanwhile, the needs evaluation had changed some of our thinking about how to implement the project. Originally we thought that, like the hotel systems we developed, the RM function would be performed in the field offices, since they had profit-and-loss responsibility. In time, however, we concluded that National had to get control faster; it simply couldn't take the time to educate all the field managers. It needed a hard-core group of RM fanatics who would get this thing off the ground. Above all, National needed a strong-willed, intensely focused champion who would have the authority to cut through organizational politics and get the work done. The most important decision National made was putting the right man in the job. Ernest Johnson, who had been promoted to vice president of Revenue Management in January 1993, was involved in the project from the start.

Ernest didn't have the traditional background of people who go into RM. A "typical youth of the rebellious sixties," Johnson had earned a couple of degrees in German literature and had taught German and English to mining executives in Andalusia, Spain. Later, he was involved in the commercial production of jojoba oil for the cosmetics industry. Johnson's entrepreneurial bent led him to work for Hertz Rent-a-Car in Fresno, California, where he returned that station to profitability. Hertz promoted him to supervisor of the company's northern Nevada locations, where he encountered fluctuating demand cycles and started experimenting with price differentials that corresponded to demand shifts. At the time, Hertz was beginning a project it called "Yield Management" and was looking for a test site. Johnson signed on for Reno and used a system that attempted to match pricing to demand. Reno soon experienced significant improvement in revenue and fleet utilization during low-demand periods.

In 1987, Johnson joined National as a regional vice president; in 1989 he moved to National headquarters as vice president of international operations. By the time Vince Wasik left National, Johnson had a good idea of National's operations both domestically and internationally; he had also been involved in the RAT and RAM strategy. He had a good grasp of the demand and pricing issues and was keenly interested in Revenue Management. He spearheaded the search for a Revenue Management consultant and systems builder and developed a thorough understanding of all the issues National had to resolve to incorporate RM into its business. Johnson fought for the chance to lead the RM project, ready to roll up his sleeves and do what it took to get the job done. He believed in the project and was determined to be a part of it.

Once in place, Johnson received the full support of senior management. He was a strong leader, and he took the flak when people in the organization resisted cultural changes or when naysayers and skeptics put up roadblocks. With our help, he attacked three major issues: the need to centralize the RM function and authority at headquarters; the design and construction of the RM organization, including all necessary training; and the education of field, reservations, and corporate people on National's RM strategy and goals.

The first critical decision involved where to put the Revenue Management function. "The easiest thing would have been to advocate a decentralized function," says Johnson. "That would have been politically easy and culturally simple, because it did not mean significant change. But we just couldn't get around the fact that Revenue Management had to be centralized. We kept coming back to the point that it can't be just pricing. It had to be *pricing and inventory together* because the huge opportunity was in the inventory." Johnson recognized that people in local airport offices are necessarily focused on things like operational needs and customer service. He could put revenue controllers in the field offices, but, realistically, they would be called upon to do other things of an operational nature, taking their focus away from Revenue Management responsibilities. He also realized that the opportunity for ongoing training and sharing of knowledge would be limited if revenue controllers were isolated in offices around the country.

About three-fourths of the Revenue Management organization came from inside National. Johnson selected the staff from several disciplines, including the finance department, the insurance department, and field operations. "They had to have cerebral power, be good analytical thinkers, handle lots of stress, be able to take risks, and be accountable for the results. These are people who were challenged intellectually and professionally by being a part of the RM project. The learning curve is like a rocket that goes straight up. You need people with open minds who are willing to break with everything they have been taught before." To fill out the rest of the staff, Johnson advertised in Chicago, Minneapolis, Atlanta, and Dallas, the locations of major airline offices and their RM departments.

A few days before we turned the Phase .5 system on, when we were in the final stages of testing, I was sitting by one of the revenue controllers responsible for the Los Angeles market. We were testing the system for his market, and when he saw the forecast produced by the RM system, he exclaimed,

"My strategy has been backwards! On this week, I've been holding the line on prices, and on that week, I was discounting. Now it's flip-flopped." With Phase .5 installed, the machine was producing forecasts that were counterintuitive. Still, he was willing to change the way he had thought about the market. In time, his leap of faith proved justified.

HITTING A SNAG

The pressure on the RM team was high throughout the project, but the first couple of months were especially intense. Ramaekers kept pressing us to do things faster, and we kept running into problems. It was a brutal environment. Tim Hart and the rest of our team were working twenty hours a day, seven days a week. The project became known as "the widowmaker." Even without any unanticipated problems, the development schedule was too ambitious, but we encountered several obstacles we hadn't anticipated. First, National wanted an enhancement to the Phase .5 system that was not part of the original plan. It wanted the ability to update rates in the in-house and global distribution systems instantaneously. Second, the volume of data that had to be processed had been underestimated. An enormous amount of data had to be transported to the RM platform every day, where it was processed to produce the forecasts and rate/inventory recommendations for each location; then, these recommendations had to be transferred back into the reservations systems.

This problem came into sharp focus when we were hit by what we called "the Gupta bug." We had chosen Gupta database software for the Phase .5 system after being impressed by a benchmark test for another client. It was a nice little database engine that had some great tools for rapid development.

As we learned the hard way, though, the key word here was "little." We knew the National database was going to be big, and all the Gupta literature indicated that the software could handle large databases. As soon as it was installed, however, the database caused a number of LAN crashes as we tested the Phase .5 system. These crashes were serious, affecting every system connected to the LAN. Worse, the restoration of service was awkward.

We contacted the Gupta people about our problem, and the first thing they asked was, "How big is the database?"

"Well, right now, it's 1 gigabyte but it will go to 3 to 5 gigabytes," we told them.

"Whaaaat??" they replied.

"How do you handle it?" we asked.

"We don't know. We don't have any other systems this big."

Basically, the message was that we were on our own.

Our difficulty with the Gupta database caused tremendous problems, not the least of which was a major confrontation with Larry Ramaekers. By now, it was obvious that we were not going to make the original July 4 deadline for Phase .5. Ramaekers was leaning hard on the team because he was convinced that National had to get Phase .5 up and running for the peak summer season. Finally, we managed to get the system stabilized. We assigned two of our people to baby-sit it constantly. They ran checks on the databases in the morning and at night, and they backed everything up so that if the bug crashed the system, we could restore it quickly. By mid-July, Phase .5 was functional, though far from perfect. But it produced some good results right away.

Throughout August, the system was up and down, and Ernest Johnson was facing a board meeting at which he was scheduled to demo the Phase .5 system. Although we had made great progress in working around the Gupta problem, we didn't want to trust it for this critical presentation. There was still a danger that the board would get cold feet and pull the plug on this expensive project, so we built a stand-alone PC version for the demonstration. In the end, this backup was not needed—the demo went very well. By the time the meeting was over, the board members were really committed to Revenue Management, which gave the project a lot of credibility with GM.

Soon after the demo of Phase .5, the GM representative on the National board came to National headquarters for a couple of days. He wanted a fuller demonstration of the system because it was going to be one of the crown jewels that would enhance the selling price for National. Ernest Johnson walked him through the entire system, and he got tremendously excited. He had never seen anything like it and couldn't believe that the system could forecast and make rate recommendations with such accuracy. He was amazed that pressing one button automatically updated the prices and availability in National's reservations system and that all the travel agency systems that sold National's products received the changes overnight. This was just Phase .5, but it was slick and did a lot of great things that no other car rental company could do.

During his visit, the GM guy asked, "How long does it take for the rates and inventory availability to go from here to a display in the reservations network?"

Ernest pressed the button that forwarded the rates and then picked up the phone and dialed National's 800 reservations number. "Go ahead, ask the res agent," he said.

The GM guy did, and he was quoted the new rate. He was flabbergasted. But this was nothing compared with what the Phase 1 system would deliver nine months later.

The Gupta bug nearly derailed the project, but it was not the only challenge we faced. We had to fight constantly with technical people who wanted to hold up the system—sometimes for trivial reasons such as changing the font parameters or the size of the cursor. Keeping everyone focused on the main objective of getting the system into production was a challenge, even though we all knew how critical the situation was. This was a very complex system, and getting all its pieces to work together smoothly was no easy task. And smooth wasn't good enough—we had to get it to run *fast*, because in Revenue Management, time is money. Reacting quickly to changes at the micromarket level is where the real benefit of RM lies.

Once everything was in place in Phase 1—the hardware, the software, the people, and the processes—National began seeing major improvements in revenue. The Phase 1 RM machine was crunching 30 gigabytes of data every night, analyzing historical booking and pricing patterns, and looking at future bookings. It was forecasting the demand for every city, every car class, and every price level for sixty days into the future; prioritizing future days that had high revenue opportunity; it was making recommendations on how to manage the inventory and rates. In other words, it was doing exactly what it was designed to do.

SUCCESS!

The National experience was like riding a roller coaster. It was exciting and sometimes scary during the ride, and we all felt great relief when it was finally over. The pressures were tremendous, and problems that are routine in other software development projects—like bugs in the programs, minor delays, additional testing, and internal politics—took on crisis proportions because so much was at stake.

The stress was soon justified by the results, which were

spectacular. The Phase .5 system had provided improvements while giving us time to develop the Phase 1 power machine. Larry Ramaekers began to acknowledge that the program was working when he saw the September 1993 revenue results. Car rental firms make money fairly easily in July and August, but the September figures convinced him that National would be making money for the year. The improved performance continued the following year, too. In November 1994, Ramaekers looked back on the turnaround with evident satisfaction. "In 1994, we will make a profit that by anybody's calculation is a respectable profit—not just for the car rental business, but a profit that would be acceptable to anybody. This company, which had been relatively stagnant in sales, is now growing at 19%."

The growth was not just financial, either. In the cost-cutting days, National had cut its fleet down to sixty thousand cars under the premise that cutting costs made money. The Revenue Management system enabled National to increase the fleet to one hundred thousand cars, because it could effectively manage this larger fleet. Additionally, the company saw improved results in airport rentals. In Los Angeles, for example, National's share of airport business in April 1995 increased from 11.4% to 14.82% (compared with April 1994), while Alamo's share dropped from 22% to 19% and Avis's dropped from 20% to 18%. National's share increased at most other airports as well.

In June 1995, General Motors completed the sale of National Car Rental System to a seasoned group of car rental executives headed by William Lobeck, who had been president of Chrysler's Pentastar Group. On June 6, I received a letter from Larry Ramaekers in which he acknowledged our contribution during the turnaround. "The Revenue Management system that you and the Aeronomics team developed is a major part of the National success story." Larry had been a tough customer, and we butted heads on more than one occasion, but he had supported the project from the beginning and stayed the course through the tough times.

In 1996, INFORMS/CPMS, an organization comprising operations research professionals throughout the world, named the National Car Rental RM program one of five finalists for the prestigious Franz Edelman Award, the Heisman Trophy of the operations research world. This distinguished award recognizes exceptional use of mathematical and scientific techniques to solve problems in government, military, corporate, and industrial applications around the world. Inclusion in this competition represented a major validation of the Revenue Management theory, process, and system.

8

WHAT YOU DON'T KNOW ABOUT REVENUE MANAGEMENT COULD KILL YOU!

I got led down the river more than once. I honestly believed I knew what was happening in information technology. So, for someone who doesn't know about Revenue Management today . . . My God!
—DONALD BURR, CHAIRMAN AND CEO,
PEOPLEEXPRESS AIRLINES

RM AS A COMPETITIVE WEAPON

IN PREPARATION FOR WRITing this book, I conducted a survey of CEOs on the Fortune 500 list to determine the awareness level of RM in the business community. The survey asked recipients if they knew about Revenue Management as a competitive weapon, gauged their level of understanding of this new management science, and requested basic information about their company's supply, demand, and pricing issues.

When the survey was taken, in August 1992, Revenue Management was an established force in the airline and hotel industries, and the discipline was beginning to migrate to trucking, television broadcasting, and a few other industries. There had been a number of articles on RM in business and trade journals, including a story in the *Wall Street Journal* about the RM successes at Delta. But I still didn't have a good sense of the level of knowledge about Revenue Management to properly position this book in the general business community.

I sent the survey to two groups of companies. Group I was composed of companies in industries where RM was already an accepted practice. Members in this group responded enthusiastically. They understood the power of RM and were hungry for more information about it. They also saw the potential for RM in other industries. Group II comprised one hundred CEOs in a wide range of industries, including chemicals, food manufacturing, telecommunications, pharmaceuticals, publishing, tobacco, and petroleum refining. All these industries wrestle with the seven uncertainties that Revenue Management addresses. I was amazed when the replies indicated that not a single person in this group was aware of RM and its ability to generate more revenue.

At the time the survey was conducted, the abysmal 1991 financials were still sending shock waves down Wall Street. Among the Fortune 500 industrials, 1991 profits had fallen 41%, and 103 of these companies had reported losses. Only one in the top ten reported a profit increase. In boardrooms everywhere, companies were urged to review the mistakes and excesses of the past decade, make fundamental changes in their organizations, and gear up for fiercely competitive times ahead. For the next few years, frenzied cost-cutting and downsizing spread like wildfire. Nobody seemed to think that growth in the market was a possibility that should even be addressed.

But now, the downsizing mania has lost its appeal, and

concerns about the need for real growth are surfacing again. That's why Revenue Management has been identified as one of the most important tools a company can use to promote revenue growth at minimum risk. In early 1996, for instance, the *Wall Street Journal* zeroed in on RM, listing it first among four important emerging business strategies and observing that Revenue Management is "poised to explode."

In today's entropic marketplace, every business should be aware of the potential of RM as a competitive weapon. What Don Burr didn't know about RM killed PeopleExpress. Even when he read about RM in the airline trade magazines, Burr did not realize its potency. In a 1985 issue of *Lloyd's Aviation Economist* was an article about the work that I was doing in what was then called Yield Management. That issue also included an editorial suggesting that Yield Management might be the only way for the established airlines to compete effectively against the low-cost airlines such as PeopleExpress until they could get their costs under control. Burr responded with a guest editorial in the next issue in which he dismissed Yield Management as an old concept that had merely been dressed up to show that the major airlines were doing something to respond to the competitive threat of PeopleExpress. He did not understand the level of sophistication to which these concepts had been taken through advances in computerization and mathematical modeling. Burr later admitted that this misunderstanding was a fatal error.

Those who know of the power of RM as a competitive weapon can often recognize it when it has been turned on them. I recently received a phone call from the senior vice president of marketing at a major hotel chain. I had worked with his company a few years ago, and he had seen the power of RM in helping him with market penetration. Now he was seeing another chain take market leadership just as he had a few years back. "Are you working with them?" he asked.

"You know I can't tell you." I replied.

"You don't have to," he said. He knew what was happening. An experienced RM professional, he recognized that RM was giving the competitor the ability to compete more effectively against him.

OF SHAMS AND SHAMANS

Almost as deadly as ignorance of Revenue Management are misguided or misinformed RM efforts. This misdirection can come from internal roadblockers who seem to be supporting an RM initiative but are in fact resisting or misusing it. It can also come from external shamans who profess to understand RM and mislead innocent victims. Both can be devastating.

One story illustrating internal misdirection involves PanAm, which was effectively the U.S. flag carrier for decades. The airline had fallen on hard times as the skies opened to more competition. In February 1986, Tony McKinnon was appointed executive vice president at PanAm. I had worked with Tony when we were both at Delta, and he brought my firm in to see if we could help turn PanAm around. It was a daunting task; revenue was just one of many serious problems. Nevertheless, we put together some organizational procedures and databases to help identify and capture revenue opportunities. The computer system we installed did not have forecasting and optimization features, but it had some clever "flagging" features that identified revenue opportunity. In the first year, our efforts had a positive revenue impact of $70 million. But it was not enough—by then, PanAm was losing $200 million per year.

McKinnon left PanAm to take a senior marketing position at American Airlines just as we were proposing to move

PanAm to the next step and install forecasting and optimization. After McKinnon's departure, however, the RM staff at PanAm decided to go in a different direction. They purchased a PC-based system that was not nearly large enough to handle PanAm's extensive route network. About a year later, PanAm's new senior management team called us in to evaluate what they were doing with RM. PanAm's revenues had gone down since the purchase of the system, and management was afraid that the new system was providing erroneous recommendations.

"We have good news and bad news," we told them after our review. "The good news is that the system is not costing you any money. The bad news is that it has not even been put into production." As it happened, the PC system was not giving acceptable recommendations, but that hardly mattered since the system was never put into daily use because it could not handle the volume of data. Trying to pump all the data through the system on a nightly basis caused the hardware to overheat and the system to crash. No one could get the system to work reliably. The system vendor had even tried pulling the cover off the PC chassis and positioning a fan to blow directly on the circuit boards.

When we told the senior executive this, he asked sarcastically, "What are you saying? We need bigger fans???"

Bigger fans wouldn't have helped. Within a year or so, PanAm was out of business. I was told later that the PC system had never been put into production, which was probably just as well.

As awareness of Revenue Management increases in the business community, there will be more and more people who proclaim themselves experts at RM tactics. Inevitably, some of them will be anything but experts. But it's difficult for companies with no RM knowledge to know the difference, and some hire people with questionable RM credentials. It's like having a one-eyed king in the land of the blind.

A major transportation company decided to get into RM and engaged a multinational consulting firm to help design and develop an RM program. After spending millions of dollars and more than a year of effort, the consulting firm had come up with only design specifications. I was asked to review the specifications, so I took a stack of material home and late one evening began to read the binder labeled "Revenue Management System—Summary Overview." It included high-level requirements, flow charts, and database designs, but it didn't make much sense to me. I thought that I was just tired, so I got some coffee and sat down again with the book. Before long, it became clear that this was not a *Revenue Management* system—it was a *Revenue Accounting* system. The company was going to collect and process enormous amounts of customer data at the micromarket level, but there was no attempt to segment markets, forecast demand, optimize response, or do anything I would call RM other than report historical demand. The consulting firm had delivered all they really knew—revenue accounting.

On another occasion, we were asked to review an RM system that had just been installed at a hotel. The hotel was testing the system and was not satisfied with the results, but it didn't know what was wrong. Within a few minutes, we figured it out. The logic for the price recommendations was not driven by the principles of RM—it was tied to the objective of meeting predetermined budget targets. If there was strong demand for a particular night, and it looked like the budget would be met, the system recommended that rates be reduced. If there was weak demand, it recommended that the rates be raised for any additional guests. In both cases, the system was proposing exactly the opposite of good RM tactics. In general, you need to charge more in periods of high demand and discount more when demand is weak. Fortunately, the hotel never implemented the system.

PITFALLS—CLASSIC MISTAKES IN RM STRATEGIES

For a large number of companies, Revenue Management has generated hundreds of millions of dollars. Revenue gains of 3%–7% are often realized with relatively little incremental cost. For other companies, however, the gains have been elusive. In some cases, the Revenue Management program never got off the ground, or, if it did, there were no measurable benefits. What distinguishes those with dazzling revenue gains from those that plod along?

It may appear that many things can prevent a company from reaping the full benefit of RM, but in fact there is a relatively small number of classic mistakes made by those who adopt RM techniques. In RM projects, as with virtually any other project, it is critical to keep potential pitfalls in mind. Forewarned is forearmed. Knowledge of these pitfalls can help avoid failure.

PITFALL #1: FAILURE TO QUANTIFY BENEFITS

- **Pitfall**—The company does not take the time and effort to quantify the expected benefit to be gained from implementing Revenue Management or enhancing an existing RM program. Management assumes that there is sufficient value to proceed, and the mentality is to "just do it." Without knowing where the revenues are and how they can be captured, focus on the project is soon lost, and the many other real and immediate issues facing management eventually take precedence over the vague promise of future revenue gain.

- **Avoiding the Pitfall**—Prior to initiating a Revenue Management program or embarking on a significant enhancement to an existing one, an in-depth evaluation of the expected benefit must be undertaken. Techniques such as simulation analysis should be used to answer such questions as: How much revenue can we expect to gain? How can it be achieved? What is the impact of real-world constraints? This exercise should result in a consensus from all those affected, and the projected revenue-per-year increase should be used as a motivational target to keep everyone focused when the inevitable difficulties arise.

PITFALL #2: LACK OF A WELL-DEFINED PLAN

- **Pitfall**—Clear operational objectives are not specifically established, and no road map of how to proceed is developed because of the eagerness and urgency that the RM potential creates. Roles and responsibilities of the players are unclear, and turf wars result. The company soon finds that raw energy and enthusiasm are no substitute for a coherent and disciplined process.
- **Avoiding the Pitfall**—Time must be taken to build a common vision for the Revenue Management project. The objectives must be put in writing and published for

all those affected. Time frames must be established, and specific roles and responsibilities of all individuals must be identified. A champion with broad authority over and responsibility for the success of the project is essential to ensure that the project stays on track.

PITFALL #3: LACK OF SENIOR MANAGEMENT OVERSIGHT

- **Pitfall**—After approving a Revenue Management project and authorizing the expenditure of resources, senior managers often become involved in other issues that seem to be more urgent but are in fact less important. With senior managers' attention shifted to other topics, failure to follow up on the RM project is interpreted as a lack of interest in the outcome, and corporate focus is lost. Eventually, the workforce perceives RM as just another fad. Without senior management's unswerving commitment, many obstacles come up that can derail an RM effort.
- **Avoiding the Pitfall**—The roles of senior managers must be well defined at the beginning of the project. Frequent briefings must be scheduled, and senior management must monitor results, not effort. Issues that may obstruct or delay the program must be resolved. Additionally, senior managers must continually encourage people to take the next step on the path to revenue maximization. After all, RM is a continuous process—not a one-time event.

PITFALL #4: PARALYSIS BY ANALYSIS

- **Pitfall**—Revenue Management prompts some companies to form ongoing study groups and generates lots of "white papers." This approach most often emerges when those charged with the RM task seek to come up with "the ultimate RM solution." Since RM is a rapidly evolving discipline, this is impossible. Any task force that attempts to assess all the new Revenue Management techniques as they evolve will find itself chasing its tail and getting nowhere.
- **Avoiding the Pitfall**—Members of the group charged with implementing Revenue Management or RM enhancements must set and achieve short-term goals even as they work on developing a long-term plan. The team must focus on business requirements, not technology. While RM technology has been changing rapidly, a company's business requirements are more stable. Often those requirements can be met without the latest in RM technology. Revenue from short-term improvements can fund the long-term direction.

PITFALL #5: VIEWING THE SYSTEM AS THE SOLUTION

- **Pitfall**—Since it is often the most visible aspect of a Revenue Management program, the RM computer system can overshadow the equally important aspects of organization, staffing, and procedures. Dealing with the required organizational, personnel, and process changes can be painful and difficult, yet these elements are often given short shrift.

• **Avoiding the Pitfall**—Revenue Management is a business philosophy, and the computer system is only a tool (albeit an important one) that facilitates the RM philosophy. Thus the RM champion must be a talented manager and an experienced businessperson, not a technician, no matter how big the system issues appear to be. The champion must focus on all the elements required for the successful implementation of the RM program, and success should be measured not by the implementation of a computer system but by the generation of incremental revenue. Of course, quick gains can often be obtained simply by adopting an RM attitude and changing certain policies or practices that obviously inhibit the maximization of revenue.

PITFALL #6: FAILURE TO MEASURE REVENUE PERFORMANCE

• **Pitfall**—So many variables, both internal and external, affect a company's revenues that some managers assume that the gain from Revenue Management cannot be isolated and measured. They are wrong. Without a way to measure revenue gain specifically from RM, companies may lose focus on the RM objectives. Other metrics (such as revenue per unit sold, sales volumes, or computer system milestones) are substituted, and although they may be valid indicators of success, they do not directly grade the RM effort.

- **Avoiding the Pitfall**—Specific revenue targets should be set for the company as a whole, as well as for individual market segments and revenue managers. The targets must be attainable and reasonable within the control of the RM group. Thanks to sophisticated simulation techniques, it's possible to isolate the impact of RM actions versus other factors. Use of revenue opportunity models that measure remaining potential revenues will keep the group focused on continual revenue improvement.

PITFALL #7: HELD HOSTAGE BY TECH-HEADS

- **Pitfall**—In extreme cases, the technical people take over the system development and refuse to release it to users until it meets their criteria, which are sometimes arbitrary. I've seen systems that could generate tens of millions of dollars waiting on acceptance by technical people because the cursor blinks too fast or the screen displays all uppercase letters rather than upper- and lowercase. In one situation, the technical staff made the arbitrary decision that the response time for any screen display would be no greater than seven seconds. They held up acceptance of a system for months because one screen took ten seconds to display. Since this was the primary screen the users would access, and since they would use this screen over one hundred times a day, the techies concluded that the average user would "waste" over five minutes a day. During these ten seconds the system was performing sophisticated data modeling, and the average screen revealed $800 in incremental revenue. That was $80,000 in daily revenue they were foregoing to save the user five minutes of wait time!

- **Avoiding the Pitfall**—The opportunity cost of not having the RM system in place should be known to everyone on the project, even the computer technicians. The person who has the authority and responsibility for revenue generation should set the standards for acceptance from a user's standpoint, and the main criterion should be whether the company could make more money with the system than without it.

PITFALL #8: LACK OF A COHERENT MARKET SEGMENTATION PLAN

- **Pitfall**—RM success depends on understanding and forecasting demand at the micromarket level. Markets that are not properly segmented cannot be properly isolated and targeted with specific products and RM tactics. Some companies, however, have a tendency to segment the market based on the way they perceive it, not the way the customer behaves. Customers in the amoeba market will move in and out of micromarkets as the circumstances of time and place dictate, and the RM-driven company must respond accordingly.
- **Avoiding the Pitfall**—An in-depth review of the marketplace and the segmentation of various submarkets is required to understand the price sensitivities and buy-

ing profiles of the different market segments. Only after this analysis is complete can products be positioned and priced right for the appropriate micromarkets. Discounted products must be targeted to micromarkets where incremental sales will be made. They should have suitable characteristics (such as being available only on Tuesday) that will not inconvenience customers in the targeted micromarkets but will be effective barriers to customers willing to pay more.

DOWNSIDE RISKS

Like any powerful tool, RM can be tremendously beneficial or it can be dangerously destructive. My colleague Steve Swope likens RM to a power saw. Use it properly and you can build better houses much faster. Use it improperly and you can saw your hand off before you know it.

Bob Crandall, chief of American Airlines, understands how important it is to use the RM tools properly—after all, it's worth $500 million a year to his company. An incident at American in the mid-1980s illustrates why Crandall is so insistent on being kept in the RM loop.

With the continuing development of its hub and spoke route system, the operations research department at American Airlines realized the need to identify the revenue contribution difference between local point-to-point passengers and passengers connecting to other flights on the American system through a hub. It was a complicated RM systems issue, but finally a new control technique called "virtual nesting" was developed to ensure that the highest-revenue-producing passengers were allocated seats on flights that were projected to be full. For example, a passenger requesting a seat on a high-demand flight from Austin to Dallas so that he could connect to an American flight to Tokyo would be given precedence for a seat over a passenger who wanted the Austin–Dallas segment only.

Crandall knew the project was under development, but he had not been advised of the proposed installation date. One day, he learned from a routine report that virtual nesting was about to be installed in the reservations system. Crandall realized that virtual nesting would mean major changes in how American viewed its business and controlled the passenger booking process. He insisted on being briefed before the new system was activated. He wanted to understand how it was going to behave in the market and to ensure that all bases had been covered.

A data processing manager was sent to explain the system to Crandall, but he couldn't answer Crandall's questions on the business issues. Now Crandall was nervous, so he scheduled another meeting and required that it be attended by everyone involved in this project. Crandall's conference room is dominated by a round table so big that it requires shuffle board sticks to pass paper across it. In this intimidating setting, with about thirty people looking on, a relatively new marketing executive made an attempt to explain the new system to Crandall. Again Crandall asked a number of very pointed questions about how the company intended to manage its business in this new environment. But he still didn't get satisfactory answers. According to people who attended this meeting, the presenter got flustered while attempting to explain the internal control mechanisms in the software and finally said something like, "Well Bob, it's like this. We just turn this big knob up or we turn this big knob down, and that's how we control it."

By this time, Crandall had had enough. Sitting on the edge

of his seat, with his sleeves rolled up, he began pounding the table and reportedly shouted, "I don't want to hear about your fucking knobs. I want to know how you intend to run this thing. You don't understand. If you do this thing wrong, you could take this airline into the tank and it ain't never coming back!"

Crandall was right. They weren't ready. He made them go back and do a detailed simulation analysis of how the new system would work and what kind of decision support systems were needed. It took about a year to get it right. This time, Crandall got a four-hour, highly detailed presentation on all the relevant business and operational issues. Only then was virtual nesting finally turned on. "You know, nothing can screw things up as fast as a computer," says Crandall in explaining why he stays involved in Revenue Management projects. "When we turn the sucker on, it can sell a million tickets before you can say 'jack rabbit,' and once you've sold them, you've got to carry the people. You cannot afford to make mistakes in systems that are as integrated as this where the leverage is so great."

More than once, Crandall learned this lesson the hard way. In 1988, a computer glitch in American's RM system cost the company at least $50 million in lost ticket revenue in the second quarter. The system recommended closing out discount seats on certain flights when, actually, plenty of discount seats should have been made available. Callers requesting advertised low-fare seats were turned away and referred to competitors. American had installed new software to improve revenues, but the software had not been fully tested and it closed off the selling of discount seats prematurely in the reservations system. At the time, more than half of American's seats were in the discount category. The glitch was discovered when American's load factors for the period were not only lower than American had expected but lower than those of most of American's competitors, signaling that something was obviously not right. You can bet that Bob Crandall got the problem fixed in a hurry.

Introducing something as all-encompassing as Revenue Management to an organization is a challenging process, but it can bring great rewards to the organization and the people in it. As entropy in the marketplace continues to increase, the key to future success is dynamic decision making on the micromarket level. This involves the entire organization, and it requires cross-functional communication, focused understanding of the company's objectives, speed and connectivity, and checks and balances. Revenue Management—the attitude, processes, and systems—can take companies to greater revenue growth.

THE ETHICS OF REVENUE MANAGEMENT

The practice of Revenue Management often contradicts traditional "first come, first served" business policies, which lead some people to ask whether RM falls within the bounds of "fair" business practices. Is it ethical, for instance, to turn away willing customers in favor of saving your product for others who will be willing to pay more at a later time?

People who are otherwise fervent capitalists are often uncomfortable with the concept of segmenting customers based on their willingness or ability to pay. My friend Carol Meinke was initially afraid that it would be unfair to charge her Saturday customers more than other customers. Even consumers who benefit tremendously from the practice of Revenue Management sometimes question it. Some of Carol's customers did grumble about paying more for Saturday haircuts, but most liked having price options.

Airlines, in particular, have taken a lot of heat for their complex pricing practices. Passengers who are able to fly on discounted tickets for far less than the average cost of a seat often complain about restrictions such as advance purchase or about the fact that they could not get a discount seat on the particular departure they wanted. Businesspeople complain that they are "subsidizing" low-fare tickets; they believe their average ticket price would go down if fares were raised for the discretionary traveler.

Most business passengers don't understand that airlines forecast demand for late-booking, full-fare passengers and literally "save" seats for them. I was recently on a Delta flight from New York's La Guardia Airport to Atlanta, and I was sitting next to a man who was obviously very upset. He fumed, "I hate these bastards. I hate them." I asked him what he was talking about. He said, "I'm paying six hundred bucks for this flight, and last week, I flew all the way to the West Coast for six hundred bucks." The rest of the conversation went something like this:

"What do you think you should pay?"

"About half that."

"When did you buy your ticket?"

"Yesterday."

"Look around this flight. This is a peak Friday afternoon flight from La Guardia to Atlanta. This plane is chock-a-block full. Do you see any empty seats?"

"No."

"If Delta had a half-price sale going on and charged three hundred bucks for all these seats, do you think they would have had any seats left to sell to you yesterday?"

"Well, I guess not."

"You probably could have booked a deep discount fare two weeks ago."

"My plans changed yesterday."

"You could have gone Saturday morning or later tonight and gotten a discount."

"I didn't want to go tomorrow morning. I wanted to go home today on this flight."

That's the point. He got exactly what he wanted, when he wanted it. Sure, he paid more than he would have liked, but he got a seat on the flight that he wanted at the last minute.

What my outraged seatmate couldn't understand is that business customers and discretionary travelers are two completely different market segments. Each passenger segment benefits, and so does the airline. The discount passenger benefits from having access to seats that would have otherwise flown empty at a price far less than the *average* cost of the seat but for more than the incremental cost of flying the passenger. They are willing to change flights, departure times, departure days, or even destinations to get the fare they want. Discount fares cover the incremental cost of the passenger, as well as some of the airlines' fixed costs. Accordingly, contrary to what most business travelers believe, if the deep discount fare passengers were not on board, business fares would rise!

Business travelers want a seat available at the last minute, and they are willing to pay more for it. The revenue-maximizing airline will save seats for the last-minute, high-fare passenger. In this case, the airline takes the risk that the seat flies empty if no one wants it at the last minute for a premium price.

This entire process can be viewed as a risk-shifting exercise. The airline is willing to sell some of its seats at deep discounts to passengers who book early, reducing the airlines' risk that those seats will go empty. If the passenger is willing to buy a nonrefundable ticket to get a tremendously deep discount, he or she assumes all the risk for the seat revenue. Of course, the airline can't afford to shift all the risk at this low rate, and it gladly assumes the risk of some empty seats by saving seats for the last-minute, premium-fare business traveler.

The point is, Revenue Management gives consumers a wider range of options. It isn't unethical for businesses to charge different rates for the same product because, in fact, the product often isn't the same. For instance, a hotel room available thirty days in advance when the hotel is half booked is not the same product as a hotel room saved for the last minute when there is limited inventory and peak demand. Similarly, a Saturday haircut with a two-hour wait is not the same as one with a brief wait.

What purchasers are really looking for is not just the product but the *opportunity to buy* the product under the right circumstances and at an acceptable price. Revenue Management is about demand-based pricing, and demand-based pricing recognizes the value cycle of a perishable product or service. This value cycle varies according to local-market value, day-of-week value, seasonal value, and competitive value. These elements change the perceived worth of the product or service over time. As long as you notify the customer what your different products and prices are going to be at any moment in time and explain the benefits of the pricing differentials, you shouldn't have any problems with complaints about fairness.

The ultimate arbiter of fairness is the marketplace. In these competitive times, consumers simply won't accept "unfair" practices. Public acceptance of pricing structures created by RM will be measured by acceptance in the marketplace. And despite some grumbling, customers clearly will accept pricing that isn't based on the old first-come, first-served model, as long as it is rational, understandable, and communicated properly.

ABILITIES OF THE REVENUE-DRIVEN ORGANIZATION

There is little or no grumbling, however, inside a company that has adopted the RM approach. In fact, when companies change their focus from internal cost-cutting and downsizing to external revenue, productivity and morale dramatically improve. Successive rounds of cost-cutting and downsizing send a gloomy message to both employees and customers: "We are pessimistic about our future in the marketplace, and we must take these painful steps to ensure our survival." Focusing on revenue productivity, however, sends an optimistic signal: "Our products have even more value than we realized, and the market will reward us appropriately and allow us to grow."

RM tactics encourage employees to identify revenue-generating opportunities wherever they exist. Managers and workers on the front lines become excited when they see almost instant, positive results from employing RM thinking. They begin to believe that the company can grow and that they can contribute to that growth.

In a revenue-driven organization, everyone becomes focused on improving revenue productivity from the external market. Sales, customer support, product development, finance, marketing, and operations all work together toward the goal of revenue maximization and market domination. With all personnel focused on a single objective, revenue-driven organizations are usually very well organized. Internal entropy is invariably reduced as companies significantly improve internal efficiencies in the process of becoming revenue driven. From all accounts, downsizing is turning out to be a lose–lose situation in many companies. The revenue attitude, on the other hand, is win–win for everyone.

The message of this chapter, "What you don't know about RM could kill you," applies not only to understanding the management science of RM, but also to the forces within the company that make or break RM programs. In this age of demanding shareholders, thin margins, fierce competition, and a fragmenting marketplace, the line between winning and losing, profit and loss, is very fine. RM and the additional revenue it generates can mean the difference between corporate life and death.

9

THE MARKETING
RENAISSANCE

*The customer is in charge in the new world disorder.
. . . That's why revenue maximization must start with
the customer point of view.*

—DIETER HUCKESTEIN, PRESIDENT OF THE HOTEL
DIVISION, HILTON HOTELS CORPORATION

MARKETING AT A CROSSROADS

BEFORE LAUNCHING MY
company in 1984, I did a considerable amount of research on
business start-up issues and at one point came across a quiz
that was designed to determine whether the reader was an
entrepreneur. One question in particular caught my eye:

What is the single most important element in assuring
the success of a new business?

A) Having a good idea.
B) The willingness to work hard.
C) Sufficient start-up capital.
D) Customers.

The answer is so simple and obvious. Good ideas, the willingness to work hard, and sufficient capital are important, but without customers, all three will eventually exhaust themselves. Lose sight of this and you lose the company—period. Low costs, reengineered processes, empowered employees, and cross-functional teams will not make up for the lack of a sufficient number of customers paying an appropriate price.

Understanding individual customer needs, motivations, desires, and, above all, behaviors is the essence of marketing. Today, the importance of good marketing is widely accepted, but it's worth remembering that the idea of a marketing-driven business is relatively new. For most of history, the essentials needed to survive—such as food, clothing, and shelter—were in short supply, and just about all a company had to do was produce these items, price them reasonably, and deliver them to an eagerly awaiting market. This idea of a production-driven business was the dominant model until the beginning of this century, when improved manufacturing and higher living standards resulted in a greater supply of goods than the market demanded. As competition increased, the idea of a sales-driven business—a company that concentrated on convincing customers to choose its products over those of its competitors—became the new corporate paradigm.

The 1950s postwar environment gave rise to the mass-market consumer-goods sector, which set the stage for the marketing-driven approach to business. This more sophisticated strategy required companies to conduct market research and consumer behavior studies to determine what the customer wanted, what price the customer was willing to pay, and when and where the customer wanted the product. Companies such as Procter & Gamble, Unilever, Sony, and Nike have had great success with the marketing-driven concept; they have consistently been able to anticipate customer desires, stimulate demand, and charge premium prices. Other companies have been slow to recognize the importance of good marketing and so have learned the hard way that product innovation and technology alone don't guarantee success. Failure to leverage their strengths into a dominant market position and command premium prices for their products has limited the potential of companies like Chrysler, Philips, and Apple Computer.

Today, every type of product and service business uses some level of marketing to accomplish its mission. Industries such as hospitals and other health care providers, law firms, accounting firms, banks and financial institutions, and even universities—all of which have paid minimal attention to marketing in the past—are turning up the marketing heat to survive and then win in today's increasingly competitive environment.

But here's the rub. The principles of marketing have remained relatively static for almost fifty years, but the target of these marketing techniques—the customer—is changing at an accelerating rate. The mass market is dead; niche marketing is now the order of the day. The growing entropy and disorder in the marketplace is stymieing traditional marketing concepts and methodology. Consumer behavior, once so predictable, seems to change by the minute, and the difficulty of anticipating the needs and wants of consumers is defying traditional marketing data-collection techniques like observing, surveying, and sampling. For decades, companies have relied on these techniques to make major product and pricing decisions; now, marketing departments in many companies seem ineffectual and even irrelevant.

Over the years, marketing has fought hard to gain acceptance as an important, integral, and driving force in the corporation. Marketing is often misunderstood, in large part because it's so hard to pin down. Finance, engineering, and operations executives want to see, feel, and, more important, quantify every aspect of the organization. Unless they come from a marketing background, a company's top managers often don't perceive marketing as a discipline. They are uncomfortable dealing with the subjective aspects of consumer behavior, which are usually more emotional than rational, and always undisciplined. Marketing jargon—such as synchromarketing, conjoint analysis, brand equity, effective reach, and frequency—may have significance to marketers, but these buzzwords sound fuzzy to nuts-and-bolts people like accountants, engineers, and production-line executives. To many of them, marketing is just so much fluff.

Marketers often don't help themselves in these internal struggles. Too many of them are attracted to the mind-games aspect of marketing, such as designing creative advertising or signing up celebrity spokespersons. Analysis is not their main interest, although they will use research to spark ideas or to justify or validate marketing actions. Finance, engineering, and operations all have well-defined and quantifiable objectives, but marketing initiatives more often than not begin with broad assumptions derived from blind faith or gut feel. And rarely does anyone perform a sophisticated analysis of the results of these initiatives. This puts marketing in direct conflict with finance. Finance types claim that marketers "know the value of everything and the cost of nothing," while marketers counter that finance people "know the cost of everything and the value of nothing."

Despite these difficulties, business leaders know that marketing is critical to a company's success. In the increasingly entropic marketplace, the customer is no longer king. The customer is dictator. Marketing in the amoeba market is often an expensive proposition, but strategic decisions must be made faster and faster, and the intensively competitive environment is less and less forgiving of mistakes. Investors are breathing down the necks of CEOs, demanding leaner and meaner organizations and instantaneous improvements to the bottom line. In this demanding new environment, the field of marketing— still relatively new, after all—is at an important crossroads, and there is no doubt that it must reinvent itself to meet these new challenges.

Sounds like a dire situation, doesn't it? Maybe so, yet I believe that business is on the verge of a renaissance in marketing and that Revenue Management will be the driving force.

THE MARKETING RENAISSANCE

The Renaissance that followed the Middle Ages was a period of extraordinary accomplishment in the arts and quantum advances in science. Society rediscovered the importance of the individual, and throughout this remarkable moment in history the printing press was the enabling technology that ignited discovery and diffused knowledge. Likewise, the marketing renaissance that I envision will focus on the individual and his or her distinctive needs and wants in the market. The application of science is elevating the art of marketing to new levels, and increasing computer power is the enabling technology that will make this possible.

I predict that Revenue Management will be at the center of the marketing renaissance, because RM, more than any other marketing technique, provides quantification of market opportunities before marketing initiatives are launched. With the application of core concepts and proven techniques, RM enables any company to optimize these opportunities. Its unique ability to quantify revenue results generated by marketing efforts should not only give marketers new stature in any organization but also position the revenue-driven marketing function squarely at its center. This new approach to marketing will reflect the essential characteristics of Revenue Management:

- A focus on revenue growth, not cost control
- An understanding of consumer desires and value-driven trade-offs at the micromarket level
- The ability to predict consumer behavior under particular circumstances of time and place
- The optimization of response to consumer behavior to maximize revenue
- A dynamic reevaluation of revenue opportunities in the context of the rapidly changing marketplace

For some businesses, reaping the benefits of the marketing renaissance will be largely a matter of adopting the Revenue Management attitude. Barber shops, restaurants, and other small businesses don't need rocket science mathematics to optimize responses to consumers who make perceptible price/convenience trade-offs. Revenue-maximizing opportunities can be discovered by closely observing customer conduct and gauging reactions to such tactics as price and availability changes.

For many companies, however, rapidly dividing micromarkets require the collection, manipulation, and analysis of a far greater amount of data than most companies currently use for any other function. Working at the level of individual transactions often exceeds human ability to store, sort, and interpret events and draw knowledgeable conclusions even for apparently simple situations. Take tee times at a typical golf course, for example. Let's assume that the golf course serves only five market segments, comprising avid golfers, weekend golfers, senior golfers, golf leagues, and golf tournaments. Tee times must be allocated and priced appropriately among these various segments ten months out of the year. The golf course schedules tee times at the rate of one every seven minutes for eleven hours a day. With a simple calculation, we can figure that the golf course can accommodate ninety-four groups a day, and at three hundred days of operation a year, that equals 28,200 tee times to manage per year. Those have to be allocated among five market segments, each with various price sensitivities, giving the golf course manager 141,000 decision variables, and this doesn't count variables such as seasonality, impact of weather, effect of slow or fast golfers, and other factors that alter tee-time scheduling. That's why marketing and information technology are beginning to fuel each other, and their symbiotic relationship will be at the heart of the marketing renaissance.

THE KNOWLEDGE COMPONENT

The only way companies can reduce the uncertainty in both the marketplace and the marketing process is by gathering and correctly analyzing the greatest amount of detailed information possible. Advances in computer technology are facilitating the ability to accumulate and manipulate immense amounts of data, and from this information comes the critical knowledge required to implement RM in large organizations. Companies recognize that they need greater information than ever before in every aspect of business; accordingly, they are devoting a greater percentage of their resources (as much as 10% or more) to gathering, interpreting, and disseminating data. Increasingly, the crucial question is not whether data should be gathered and converted into information but *what do you do with it once you've got it?* Revenue Management answers this question, and in the process it takes the use of corporate information technology to a new level.

Within the past decade or so, information technology has evolved from *data processing* to *information management.* Data is really nothing but raw facts and observations that are thought to be true. The amount of data available to companies has grown exponentially, and sorting and reorganizing it has ceased to be a valuable exercise primarily because the sheer volume of it overwhelms decision makers. Information, on the other hand, allows a more reasoned response. Information management collects, studies, and interprets data, transforming it into a more reliable basis for decision making. But information is not necessarily timely or accurate. Recently acquired competitive information, for example, can be materially incomplete, out of date, and misinterpreted. Information, though more useful than raw data, cannot by itself provide adequate guidance to managers and decision makers.

What's really needed is *knowledge,* which results from both observation and experience. Knowledge is higher up the evolutionary ladder than information; it is more than the collecting of facts or the interpretation of data. Knowledge comes from the ability to perceive relationships between pieces of information, construct concepts, formulate principles, and perform evaluations. While information provides a retrospective understanding of consumer behavioral patterns, knowledge provides foresight. It helps companies begin to predict what customers will do in the future. Knowledge acquired from years of experience and analysis is extremely valuable and can give a company a tremendous competitive edge.

The role of knowledge in organizations has recently become a hot button in business. In his thought-provoking book

Post-Capitalist Society, Peter Drucker describes the transformation of the economy from one based on capital and labor to one where knowledge is the basis of wealth. "Knowledge organizations," such as McKinsey & Co., Andersen Consulting, EDS, and Booz Allen, have become powerful forces in today's business world. Furthermore, the "knowledge component" in many other companies is what makes them truly valuable. Approximately one-third of the market value of American Airlines, for example, is attributable to its SABRE reservations system, although the airline has over five hundred commercial aircraft and huge facilities in major cities in the United States, Europe, Japan, and South America. Notwithstanding all these physical assets, a large portion of American's value derives from software and data residing on its computers in Tulsa, Oklahoma.

Drucker applies the term "knowledge workers" to people whose main value is the ability to gather, analyze, and disseminate information in an efficient manner. This set of people includes professionals such as lawyers, accountants, and physicians. Moreover, in virtually every organization, knowledge workers—product planners, systems designers, process engineers, advertising executives, customer service providers—add wealth to the company. Data about customers, markets, products, and competitors residing in the company's information systems also enhance the corporate body of knowledge. In a knowledge-based economy, in fact, the brainpower of workers combined with accessible information from computer systems represent a company's most valuable assets. This may be a difficult concept for business leaders to absorb and act upon when they are struggling to make profits in the heat of competitive battles, but the most successful companies will see knowledge and knowledge workers as central to all their operations.

As the knowledge component becomes a higher percentage

of the value of companies, accounting practices must change. They must give proper weight to these knowledge assets if balance sheets are to have more relevance to business leaders. The narrow focus on capital and capital assets (a holdover from the capitalist model developed a century ago) is no longer valid. In the past ten years, as the downsizing fad escalated, companies have jettisoned many thousands of people who have valuable knowledge about markets, production methods, and customers, because the knowledge these people have is not reflected on the balance sheet. Similarly, companies have thrown away valuable consumer, production, and competitive data in a myopic attempt to save computer storage space or processing time.

It is unrealistic to believe that all employees can be retained in times of economic turmoil, or that all data will be relevant in the decision-making process, but executives should ask themselves one all-important question: What do we really *need* to know? Companies, consultants, and management writers are pondering this issue of knowledge management. Some suggest creating a new corporate position, a chief knowledge officer (CKO), responsible for capturing, managing, distributing, and effectively using knowledge. They imagine this role evolving from that of chief information officer (CIO), a position that now exists in most large companies, and envision the CKO as the designer, implementer, and overseer of the knowledge infrastructure and, generally, the advocate for knowledge and learning in the organization. The underlying concept is that, if knowledge is the basis of a company's value, then companies must become "learning organizations," and the CKO would be the focal point of that educational activity. Various companies have adopted this idea, including McKinsey & Co., General Electric, Xerox PARC, and Ernst & Young.

But this idea has important limitations. Although the CIO

can help managers and other employees find information they do not have, the CIO can play only a limited role, if any, in managing the knowledge that workers already have. Nor can the CIO possibly define what needs to be known across the many disciplines that exist in most organizations. Indeed, how can any one person inventory, assign value, and protect the knowledge that resides in the brains of workers scattered across an organization? Anointing one person the chief knowledge officer is thus a misguided effort to promote the importance of knowledge to a company's performance. The acquisition of knowledge is a dynamic process that cannot and should not be managed by one person or department. It must be everyone's responsibility, and it makes no difference if the knowledge is about an internal process, a production technique, the marketplace, the competition, or any other factor related to the business. The distinctions among the tools (information systems), the toolmakers and tool maintainers (chief information officers), and the decision makers who acquire the knowledge they need and make the decisions (CEO, CFO, COO) must be clear.

GOING BEYOND KNOWLEDGE

In today's fragmented, fast-moving economy, it is no longer enough to be just knowledgeable. In simpler times, a manager's knowledge of his market could provide insight into how customers were likely to behave in the future, which would be more than sufficient to determine a course of action. Now, however, marketers must be able to predict with a much greater degree of accuracy how consumers at the micromarket level will behave today, tomorrow, and months into the future and to adjust these predictions continually. Figuring out how to efficiently satisfy movable demand—while taking into account the company's capacity, costs, competition, and distribution channels—should be a dynamic, daily process.

Knowledge is more powerful than information, but now knowledge must be taken to the next step. That step is *wisdom*. I define wisdom as *knowing what to do with the knowledge you have*. Wisdom results from the accumulation of knowledge, which in turn engenders the ability to understand situations, judge consequences of potential actions, and make sound decisions in the midst of increasing chaos. Knowledge provides an awareness of the future; wisdom lets us discern the right course of action. *Wisdom is the optimization of knowledge.*

To illustrate the concept of wisdom in business on a practical level, here is a simple example of how a company could apply the distinctions among data, information, knowledge, and wisdom:

Data: Last year, 1,227,458 battery-operated nosehair clippers were purchased in the United States. Our company's share was 88%.

Information: The male population is aging; nosehair clipper sales have trended upward over the past decade.

Knowledge: We can forecast that next year, approximately 1,440,000 battery-operated nosehair clippers will be sold in the United States.

Wisdom: We can increase production with our current plant capacity, and the market will bear a $1.25 price hike without loss of share. This will increase next year's profits by almost $1 million.

The Evolution of Information

DATA
(independent facts)

⇓

INFORMATION
(interpretation of data)

⇓

KNOWLEDGE
(assimilation of information to predict the future)

⇓

WISDOM
(optimization of knowledge to make the best decisions)

Despite all the talk about the value of knowledge, few people understand the direct link between knowledge and revenue. Decisionmakers have numerous options, even when they know with a high degree of certainty what the market will do. Wisdom guides the decision, maximizing the possible revenue. And better than any other tool or process, Revenue Management enables companies to convert data into information, information into knowledge, knowledge into wisdom, and wisdom into revenue. The progression from fact to wisdom is integral to and exemplified by the practice of Revenue Management:

Facts	yield	**Data**
Analysis	yields	**Information**
Forecasts	yield	**Knowledge**
Optimization	yields	**Wisdom**

Many organizations are exploring the edges of Revenue Management as they seek ways to use their storehouse of information and knowledge. Data mining, for example, is a relatively new technique designed to help companies discover patterns in their data. In the context of marketing, this technique facilitates the classification of consumers and the sequencing of events, such as discovering that 35% of consumers purchase a new refrigerator within one month of buying a stove. Using intensive analytical processes, some data-mining techniques are assisting in forecasting future consumer behavior. While these techniques help accumulate knowledge and can aid marketing efforts, they stop short of providing wisdom, which is required to make smart decisions based on the output.

THE DECISION MACHINES OF THE FUTURE

In the marketing renaissance, achieving optimization of knowledge (wisdom) is a discrete step. In the no-tech or low-tech world of smaller businesses, wise decision making may be a fairly simple process of gathering whatever knowledge is available to the organization and applying that knowledge to make the optimal decision. For example, a ski resort may know that because of new competition, the facility will not attract the desired number of skiers over the course of the coming season. This knowledge can be used to either cut staff to save costs or to create incentive packages to attract a larger number of skiers or other customers to the resort. The wisdom in this situation could come from the experience of employees who have observed guest behavior over many seasons, or it may come from analyses of historical data or data of similarly situated resorts. The profit-maximizing ski resort might arrive at a decision that carefully combines these options to produce the greatest amount of profit at the end of the season. This is applying wisdom to the knowledge base to make the optimal decision.

For companies facing rapidly fragmenting micromarkets, the journey from knowledge to wisdom isn't so simple and straightforward. Take, for example, a paper products manufacturer with nationwide distribution, hundreds of products, and thousands of micromarkets. Forecasting demand for each of the products is difficult enough, but then you must make decisions on when and where to discount, how much to discount, when to shift product-line manufacturing, and when to shift supply from areas of weakening demand to areas of strong demand. Now there are literally millions of decisions to be made over the course of a year. A tough proposition, even for companies that are determined to be revenue-maximizing firms. But with the powerful new decision support tools provided by RM, decision makers leading this manufacturer can handle the huge volumes of data and make the right decisions at the micromarket level. That's what it's all about in today's market, and tomorrow it will be even more critical.

Today's Revenue Management decision machines collect and filter relevant data, forecast consumer behavior, make recommendations, and present summaries in graphical format. The next generation of tools (now in progress) will do all this plus predict competitive responses and automatically respond to market conditions under circumstances classified as no-brainers. In some situations, for example, you may want to simply match a competitor's offer; in others, you may want to exploit a product advantage or a competitor's weakness to extract a premium price. Whatever the situation, these new tools will not only make it easy to access the necessary information, they will have the intelligence to anticipate the questions managers should be asking, such as: *Where is my greatest revenue opportunity?* The answers will be there before the question is asked.

More specifically, these RM-based decision machines of the future will perform the following functions:

- **External data collection and manipulation:** An inventory of all relevant data regarding customer behavior, including who purchased what product, when, where, what channel, and what price, plus competitors' products, price, and availability
- **Internal data collection and manipulation:** An inventory of all capacity data, costs, and discounts allowed and all sales, advertising, and promotion activities
- **Forecasting:** An assessment of future customer behavior by micromarket segment, including an analysis of trends, seasonality, and customer preference
- **Optimization:** A mathematical determination of the optimal action, given the constraints of capacity, cost, competition, and channels
- **Prioritization:** An ordering of the decisions required, sorted from the highest potential value to the lowest, thus prioritizing the manager's workload
- **Presentation:** A graphical interface that provides ease of access to data to validate recommendations and query data for additional market intelligence; also provides for monitoring of products, promotions, and marketing actions

Revenue Management decision machines will influence most of, if not all, the essential elements of the marketing mix. These machines are essential to the marketing renaissance; without them, large corporations will have difficulty making the leap from knowledge to wisdom in responding to market-place issues. Imagine having the ability to dynamically review market changes as they are happening. Imagine the insight these machines will provide to executives in the decision-making process. Imagine the competitive advantage that these machines (and the ability to use them optimally) will give companies in the fast-changing, increasingly competitive market. Imagine a corporate mission control group dynamically adjusting and optimizing every aspect of marketing in *planned synchronization*, including such things as these:

- **Product:** Deciding what products should be produced and in what quantities
- **Capacity planning:** Analyzing the demand and profit potential of each market segment and ascertaining what capacity should be devoted to the production of each product
- **Inventory availability:** Making a product available to a specific market segment at a certain time and deciding on the conditions under which the product will be made available
- **Price:** Determining the appropriate price of a product for each market segment for a specific moment in time and understanding the impact of this decision on revenue and profitability
- **Distribution channels:** Determining the most effective and profitable distribution channels for various market segments, including distribution via the Internet, the ultimate in one-on-one selling that heralds a return to the village marketplace, except that now the village is electronic and global
- **Promotion:** Ascertaining the right promotional mix— the most cost-effective means of advertising, promot-

ing, and selling your products to the various market segments and quantifying the returns on the promotional investment

These are not static activities. They should be managed as dynamically as the market itself is changing. Decision making needs to catch up to, and eventually get ahead of, the rate of change in the economy, competition, consumer tastes, and demographics. Developing the tools needed to facilitate effective and accurate decision making may well be the single most important challenge facing companies in the twenty-first century.

LEADING THE WAY

Who within the company will lead this marketing renaissance? In most companies, no individual has the combination of authority and responsibility for all revenue-generation activities. This prevents many RM programs from realizing their full potential (or sometimes even getting off the ground) even though the revenue opportunity has been proven in real-dollar figures.

In most modern management structures, the cost side is broken up into a number of little fiefdoms reporting to three chief officers—the chief operating officer, the chief information officer, and the chief financial officer—all reporting directly to the chief executive officer. But there is no organized revenue side corresponding to the cost side on the top officer level—a major oversight in traditional corporate structures.

Marketing initiatives, for instance, are considered to be cost activities designed to attract and sell to customers. Management gurus have been emphasizing the necessity to create "market-driven" organizations for years, yet marketing usually reports up through the chief operating officer, an individual whose job title stresses operations, a cost side function. Marketing is viewed as one of several equal activities in one division rather than the definitive activity of the entire organization.

Marketing can be easily overlooked in organizations dominated by operations and finance people. In the mid-1980s, when Sir Colin Marshall set out to transform British Airways from an operations-driven airline into a market-driven carrier, he was astonished to find that the word *marketing* was not in the title of any management-level individual in the entire organization, save for a single person in a lowly position at a remote sales office in the United States. How could British Airways become market driven if no major executive in the organization had marketing as part of his job description?

Most companies have failed to structure their organizations to reflect the importance of revenue. They have also failed to identify and study the functions that directly affect revenues. Ultimately, of course, almost everything in the organization affects revenue. Employee attitudes can either drive off or encourage demand. Production capacity and efficiency impacts revenue. Errors made by the finance department in invoicing can ruin customer relations. A market-driven company strives to ensure that everyone is attuned to the potential impact on revenue of every corporate action.

Sustained growth in corporate value can be achieved only by top-line revenue growth. But who in the final analysis should the CEO hold responsible for the top line? A chief revenue officer (CRO) position would fill this critical need. Consider an organization divided into three basic groups under the CEO—the cost (operations) group, the revenue-generation group, and the finance group, each with chief officers. The chief operating officer would be responsible for "running the factory" in an efficient and effective manner, the chief revenue officer would be responsible for all activities that generate revenue, and the chief financial officer would report on the financial status of both and provide financial services. The CEO would balance the functions within the organization to ensure the greatest return for shareholders.

Advances in simulation technology allow companies to isolate marketing factors that were not previously quantifiable. Computer simulation enables marketers to set and achieve marketing targets. This simulation ability would also permit the CEO to directly measure the performance of individual marketing factors and, therefore, also the performance of the CRO. Performance metrics could be established to demonstrate the success of the CRO in the following areas:

- **Product creation:** Have the micromarkets been properly identified and segmented, and have products been created or defined for each?
- **Pricing:** Do the prices established for the micromarkets relate to the perceived value (value cycle) each market attaches to the product at any given moment? How effective are criteria designed to restrict product availability to the micromarkets that generate the highest return?
- **Sales:** Has the sales force targeted and aggressively sold the company's products to the most valuable market segments (i.e., are they focused and measured on revenue versus volume)?
- **Advertising and promotion:** Have the expenditures on advertising and promotional activities actually generated incremental revenue? Do we know which activities generate the greatest revenue as well as the return on the investment of each activity?

- **Distribution:** Are the direct and indirect channels the most effective and profitable means of distribution?
- **Delivery:** Does the quality of the delivery positively or negatively affect the ability of the company to maximize revenues?

I recently discussed the idea of the chief revenue officer with a number of executives at several large companies. Stephen M. Wolf, the current CEO of USAir and former CEO of United Airlines and a number of other major transportation companies, hit on the basic issue immediately. "You're right," he said. "Who is the guy who focuses on the damned revenue? The chief revenue officer is a very interesting idea because frequently the marketing department gets caught up in things like a new sales brochure or advertising campaign, but nobody asks the question, 'How much money are we going to make on that sales brochure? Is it going to produce more revenue?'" He also acknowledged that putting *revenue* in the title and elevating it to senior-officer status would send a constant signal to everyone in the organization to be revenue focused.

THE REVENUE MANAGEMENT ATTITUDE: THE NEW COMPETITIVE EDGE

If your company is in the middle of cost-cutting, downsizing, and reengineering, consider this: squeezing more productivity out of people and processes in the workplace is a limiting activity. If you downsize to the point that you are cutting into the muscle of your company, you will reduce productivity rather than improve it. Such measures will yield only short-term benefits which are obtained in a negative manner. In the end, the relentless pursuit of lower costs can substantially diminish growth potential.

The Revenue Management attitude, on the other hand, is about squeezing revenue productivity from your products in the marketplace. *The potential from RM is virtually unlimited.* The RM attitude brings your company together and focuses it on growth and winning in the marketplace—positive, uplifting endeavors.

Companies that have the new competitive edge in business today have the ability to make the right decision in a split second and to understand the highly probable impact of that decision *before* it is taken. The computer simulations and real-time tracking abilities of Revenue Management provide these capabilities, and companies that know how to use these tools and relate them to the spectrum of marketing win. Competitors simply cannot overcome this advantage with conventional methods. As this becomes increasingly obvious, every company aiming to achieve market domination will realize the critical necessity of being able to monitor the daily changes in customer behavior, inventory status, pricing actions, and competitive responses on a real-time basis.

Too many companies are operating primarily with a *strategic* focus in a business world that is becoming more *tactical* by the day. Too many corporate executives are operating on tainted or incomplete information or are so overwhelmed with copious amounts of data and poorly organized information that it is all rendered useless as an aid to decision making. To win the corporate wars—and make no mistake, that is the activity in which you are engaged—you need a winning plan. Not a plan that focuses on internal processes but one that focuses on the market and competition. Not a plan that just predicts the future but one that assesses an increasingly fluid situation. Not a plan to merely make decisions but one that provides the basis for timely and effective decision making.

The writing is on the wall. Companies have been given the mandate for growth by their shareholders. In today's market, meeting this challenge head-on requires a singular focus—a *revenue* focus—around which the marketing renaissance will revolve. It will take a strong management team to transform the cost-cut, downsized, reengineered, core-competent, and confused organization into the wisdom-directed, market-dominating company that uses Revenue Management thinking, tools, and processes to direct market activities in planned synchronization. The company that succeeds in achieving this transformation and uses these tactics will have created a revenue-focused corporation. You don't want to compete against this company—you want to *be* this company.

INTERVIEWEES

The following people were interviewed or otherwise significantly contributed anecdotes, experiences, and information for this book:

Stephen P. Adkins, Director-Product Engineering, Aeronomics Incorporated

Barbara Amster, Senior Vice President–Marketing and Sales, Canadian Airlines International, Ltd.; Former Vice President–Pricing and Yield Management, American Airlines, Inc.

Peter Appel, Assistant Director–Pricing and Yield Management, Amtrak

Ben Baldanza, Senior Vice President–Pricing and Route Scheduling, Continental Airlines, Inc.

Geoff Ballotti, Director–Marketing, ITT Sheraton Corporation

Dr. Herbert Bammer, Chief Executive, Austrian Airlines

Dr. Peter Belobaba, Professor, Massachusetts Institute of Technology

Gordon Bethune, President and CEO, Continental Airlines, Inc.

Peter Bolech, Executive Vice President–Marketing, Austrian Airlines

Robert Brown, Senior Consultant, Aeronomics Incorporated

William Brunger, Staff Vice President–Revenue Management, Continental Airlines, Inc.

Keith Bryant, Business Information Controller, Forte Travelodge, UK

Donald Burr, Former Chairman and CEO, PeopleExpress, Inc.

Jim Byrd, Vice President–English Television, Canadian Broadcasting Corporation

Derek Byrne, General Manager–Europe, Aer Lingus

Gary Campbell, Executive Vice President–Customer Support, Sulcus Consulting

Jonathan Carmel, Administrative Director, Duke University Diet & Fitness Center

William Carroll, Vice President–Marketing Planning, The Hertz Corporation

Betty Chiu, Director–Sales and Special Projects, Canadian Broadcasting Corporation

Robert W. Coggin, Executive Vice President–Marketing, Delta Air Lines, Inc.

Maurice Coleman, Head of Marketing Programmes, Aer Lingus

Pat Conroy, General Manager–Information Technology, Aer Lingus

Dr. Thomas Cook, President, Sabre Decision Technologies

Robert Cotter, Senior Vice President, Director–Marketing and Product Development, ITT Sheraton Corporation

Robert L. Crandall, Chairman and CEO, American Airlines, Inc.

Gregory Cross, Corporate Director–Revenue Management, Hilton Hotels Corporation

Dr. Renwick E. Curry, Principal Scientist, Aeronomics Incorporated

Robert Dirks, Senior Vice President–Marketing, Hilton Hotels Corporation

Paul Edwards, Executive General Manager–Pricing, Scheduling & Yield, Qantas Airways Ltd.

Richard Fain, Chairman and CEO, Royal Caribbean Cruise Lines

Cameron Fellman, President, Television Bureau of Canada

John Fink, Manager–Competitive Pricing Assistance, Ford Motor Company

Robert F. Flanegin, Vice President, Aeronomics Incorporated

Robert Gall, Vice President–Marketing & Sales, Amtrak

Donald Garvett, Vice President, Simat, Hellieson & Eichner, Inc.

Chris Gibbons, Vice President–Information Technology, Microsoft, Inc.; Former Vice President–Information Technology, Promus Companies

John Gray, Managing Director–Yield Management, Southern Pacific Railroad

Julius P. Gwin, Vice President–Strategic Planning, Delta Air Lines

Phil Haan, Senior Vice President–International, Northwest Airlines, Inc.

Lawrence W. Hall, President, Aeronomics Incorporated

Stephen S. J. Hall, Executive Director, International Institute for Quality and Ethics in Service and Tourism; President, Crescent Industries; Adjunct Professor of Quality and Ethics, Institut de Management Hotelier International (France)

John Hampson, Executive Director, Forte Travelodge, UK

Richard Hanks, Senior Vice President–Sales, Marriott International, Inc.

Hollis Harris, Former Chairman and CEO, Air Canada

Timothy S. Hart, Vice President, Aeronomics Incorporated

Dieter Huckestein, President–Hotel Division, Hilton Hotels Corporation

Gordon Jack, Systems Development Manager, British Airways, PLC

Ernest Johnson, Corporate Vice President–Revenue Management, National Car Rental System, Inc.

R. Stephen Jones, Director–Marketing, Canadian Broadcasting Corporation

Dr. Alfred E. Kahn, Economist, Professor Emeritus, Cornell University; Former Senior Staff Member, President's Council of Economic Advisors; Former Chairman, Civil Aeronautics Board and New York Public Service Commission

Daniel M. Kasper, Partner, Coopers & Lybrand; Member, President's National Committee to Ensure a Strong Competitive Airline Industry

Herbert D. Kelleher, Chairman and CEO, Southwest Airlines, Inc.

Dr. Sean J. King, Senior Consultant, Aeronomics Incorporated

Ann Kirwin, Yield Manager, Aer Lingus

Craig Koch, President, The Hertz Corporation

Peter Kretz, General Manager–Marketing & Sales, Canadian Broadcasting Corporation

Robert Laird, Manager–Economics, Aer Lingus

Jimmy Legarreta, Ticket Services Director, The Washington Opera

Dr. Warren Lieberman, Senior Associate, Decision Focus, Inc.

Ray Lyons, Director–Revenue Management, British Airways PLC

Andrew P. G. Mace, Vice President, Aeronomics Incorporated

Randall Malin, President, TravelNet, Former Vice Chairman, USAir Inc.

J. Willard Marriott, Jr., Chairman and CEO, Marriott International, Inc.

Sir Colin Marshall, Chairman and CEO, British Airways PLC

Fran Marshall, Marketing Services Director, The Seven Network (Australia)

Carol Meinke, Owner, Carol's Barber Shop

Michael Morrisey, Consultant, IBM

Tom Mutryn, Vice President and Treasurer, United Airlines

Richard D. Niggley, Executive Vice President, Aeronomics Incorporated

Hans Ollongren, General Manager–Belgium; European Union Representative, Scandinavian Airlines System

Sean O'Neill, Director–Hotel & Distribution Systems, ITT Sheraton Corporation

Alvin D. Payne, Vice President, Aeronomics Incorporated

Tony Poat, Vice President–Pricing, Roadway Express

Lawrence Ramaekers, Turnaround Specialist; Interim President, National Car Rental System

Dr. Stephan Q. Regulinski, Vice President–Base Maintenance; Former Vice President-Financial Planning and Analysis, United Airlines

Brian Rice, Director–Revenue Planning & Analysis, Royal Caribbean Cruise Lines

Arturo Rodriguez, Director–Revenue Management, Aeromexico

Bruce Rowe, Director–Gaming Information Technology Development, Harrah's Casinos

Robert Santoli, Former Revenue Manager, Pan American World Airways, Inc.

Ferdinand Schmidt, Vice President for Marketing Services, Austrian Airlines

Keitha Schofield, Vice President–Information Technology, Continental Airlines

Yosef Sheffi, Director–Center for Transportation Studies, Massachusetts Institute of Technology

Dr. Julian Simon, Economist; Professor of Business Administration, University of Maryland

Barry Smith, Vice President, Sabre Decision Technologies

Derek Smith, Vice President–Strategic Planning, Sea-Land Service, Inc.

Michael Stagl, Division Manager for Revenue Management, Austrian Airlines

Kathleen Sullivan, Director–Revenue Management Systems, Hilton Hotels Corporation

Paul S. Swope Jr., Executive Vice President, Aeronomics Incorporated

Ronald Tarson, Director–Rooms, ITT Sheraton Corporation

Greg Taylor, Vice President–Revenue Management, United Airlines

Carlos Tolosa, Senior Vice President–Operations, Embassy Suites

Larry Tunison, General Manager, Radisson Park Terrace Hotel, Washington DC

John W. Wallace, Vice President, Aeronomics Incorporated

William S. Watson, Senior Vice President–Worldwide Marketing, Best Western International, Inc.

Dr. Lawrence R. Weatherford, Professor, College of Business, University of Wyoming

Stephen P. Weisz, Senior Vice President–Sales & Marketing, Marriott International, Inc.

Peter Whitford, Network Information Systems Director, The Seven
  Network (Australia)
Dr. Loren Williams, Manager–Operations Research, Aeronomics In-
  corporated
Dr. Clifford Winston, The Brookings Institution
Stephen M. Wolf, Chairman and CEO, USAir Group; Former Chair-
  man and CEO, United Airlines
Graham E. Young, Vice President, Aeronomics Incorporated

AUTHOR'S NOTE

Since the concept of Revenue Management may be new to many readers, I welcome your thoughts, comments, and impressions both on Revenue Management and the presentation of RM concepts in this book. As I prepare for my next book, I would also like to hear of your experiences, successes, and frustrations in dealing with today's continually changing marketplace.

If you are interested in further information about Revenue Management and its application, I would like to hear from you. I would also be pleased to send you information on *SCORECARD™ The Revenue Management Quarterly,* which is currently the only regularly published journal devoted to the subject of Revenue Management. Or, visit the Aeronomics home page on the World Wide Web.

Robert G. Cross
Chairman and Chief Executive Officer
Aeronomics Incorporated
Waterstone, Suite 300
4751 Best Road
Atlanta, Georgia 30337-5609

FAX: 404/763-5440
Internet: http://www.aeronomics.com
E-Mail: bob_cross@aeronomics.com

INDEX

Accountability and authority to control Revenue Management, 181–82
Accounting firms:
  perishable opportunities of, 135
  seasonal fluctuations in demand, 137, 139–40
Accounting for knowledge assets, 246
Aeronomics Incorporated, 33
Airline Deregulation Act, 34, 101
Airline industry, 3–4, 182, 215–16
  capital assets used to remedy supply/ demand imbalances, 61–62
  case study, 99–130
  databases, size of, 81
  deregulation of, 34, 100, 101, 109
  discounting to meet the competition, 153–54
  ethics of complex pricing practices, 232–34
  low-cost airlines, 34–35
    case study, 99–130
  as competitor with other forms of transportation, 9, 21, 103, 167
  PeopleExpress, see PeopleExpress
  no-shows and overbooking, 105–106, 146
  perishable opportunities of, 135
  pricing to remedy supply/demand imbalances, 65
  reservation systems, see individual airlines
  see also individual airlines
Akers, John, 18
American Airlines, 3, 34, 228–31
  case study of challenge to, and response of, 99–130
    attack of the laser fares, 116–23
    charter airlines and, 111, 112
    Dinamo (Dynamic Inventory Allocation and Maintenance Optimizer), 114, 123
    discretionary traveler, fight for, 115
    frequent flyer program, 115
    overbooking practices, 106
    SABRE reservations system, 103, 106–107, 110, 112, 115, 245
    Super Saver Fares, 112–13
    Ultimate Super Savers, 116–23, 125, 126, 129
    Value Plan, 153–54

Yield Management, 51, 112–14, 119–20, 122, 123, 125, 127–28
American Association for Nude Recreation, 15
American Express, 18
Amoeba markets, 14, 22
Amster, Barbara, 113
Analysis, overdoing, 224
Andersen Consulting, 245
Anheuser-Busch, 13
Apple Computer, 239
Appliance industry, 77
Araskog, Rand, 18
Arthur D. Little, 27
AT&T, 152
Austrian Airlines, 58–60
Authority and accountability for Revenue Management, 181–82
Automobile dealers, peak demand periods of, 137
Availability bias in interpreting data, 24

Bakeries, product wastage by, 147–48
Baldanza, Ben, 183–84
Bammer, Dr. Herbert, 59
Beer market, 13–14
Bell Labs, 97
Bennett, Tom, 198, 199
Bias in interpreting data, unintentional, 23–24, 86, 97
Book publishers, 147
Booz Allen, 245
Brand loyalty, 13
British Airways, 255
Britt Airways, 124
Broadcasting industry, 4, 14, 155, 166–67, 216
  perishable opportunities of, 135
  up front sales of ad spots, 150
Brynjolfsson, Erik, 187
Bulk purchases, competition between individual and, 149–51
Burr, Donald, 99, 100–108, 116–26, 129–30, 215, 217
Burroughs Corporation, 173–74
Business environment, unstable, 20–22
Business process reengineering (BPR), 1, 27–29, 162
Business Week, 99

Caesar's World, 18
Canadian Broadcasting Corporation
    (CBC), 3, 93–94, 155
Cancellation fees, 146, 147
Capital assets, 246
  balancing supply/demand imbalances
      with, 61–62, 138
Carmel, Jonathan, 138–39
Car rental companies, 4, 69
  competition between individual and
      bulk purchases, 149
  with first come, first served policy,
      79
  tax code changes of 1980s affecting,
      193
  see also individual companies
Case studies:
  airline industry, 99–130
  National Car Rental, 191–213
Catalog companies, peak demand
    periods of, 137
Cat food prices, 70
Champion, Revenue Management,
    179–80, 185, 225
  at National Car Rental, 205–208
Champy, James, 28
Change:
  rapid, 154–57
  resistance to, 171, 185, 198, 199,
      204–205
Charter airlines, 110–11, 112
Chief information officer (CIO), 246–
    47
Chief knowledge officer (CKO), 246
Chief revenue officer (CRO), 255–57
Chrysler Corporation, 239
Circuit City, 15
Citibank N.A., 28
Civil Aeronautics Board (CAB), 110
Clausius, Rudolf, 9
Clothing stores, 91
Coggin, Robert, 33
Commercial real estate firms:
  competition between individual and
      bulk sales, 150–51
  discounting to meet competition, 152
Communications throughout the
    organization about Revenue
    Management, 184
Compaq Computers, 82–83
Competing for the Future (Hamel and
    Prahalad), 11
Competition:
  discounting to meet, 151–54
  Revenue Management as competitive
      weapon, 215–18

stealth, 21
Compton, Jim, 94
Computer chip makers, market-based
    pricing by, 144–45
Computers, *see* Information technology
Constraints on successful Revenue
    Management program, 171–72
Consumers:
  discount mentality, 15–16
  market-based pricing and, 66–71
  nonconformist, 13–17
  predicting behavior of, *see*
      Forecasting
  value, demand for, 16
  see also Customers
Consumer surplus, 75, 143
Contests, 185–86
Continental Airlines, 123–24, 154
Core concepts of Revenue
    Management, 60–99
  continually reevaluating revenue
      opportunities, 93–96
  exploiting each product's value cycle,
      85–92
  focusing on price rather than costs,
      61–65
  making decisions based on
      knowledge, not supposition, 80–
      85
  replacing cost-based pricing with
      market-based pricing, 66–71
  saving your products for your most
      valuable customers, 77–80
  selling to segmented micromarkets,
      not mass markets, 71–77
  summary of, 61
Corporate-centric companies and
    solutions, 11, 30, 31
Cost-cutting, 1, 62, 200, 212, 216, 235
  corporate anorexia resulting from, 11
  limitations of, 1, 8, 31, 32
  transitory profits from, 8
Counterintuitive decisions, 83
Coupon promotions, 76
Crandall, Robert L., 3, 51, 99, 108–21,
    126–27, 228–31
Cruise lines, 4, 15, 132–33
CSC Index Consulting, 28
Curry, Dr. Ren, 23, 86–87
Customers, 237–38
  understanding what is being bought
      by, 167
  see also Consumers
Customization of products, 15

Data, 248, 249
  bias in interpretation of, 23–24, 86, 97
  collection of, 24, 81–82, 97, 167–68, 243–44
    in needs evaluation process, 167–68
  dissemination of, 97
  historical data, *see* Historical data, information systems making use of
  information systems to interpret, 80–85, 243–44
  information versus, 244
Data mining, 250
Dataquest, 144
Decision-making process:
  based on knowledge, 80–85
  counterintuitive, 83
  in the future, 250–54
  gut feelings in, 43, 46, 81, 106
  speed and accuracy in, 25–26, 95–96
  uncertainties in, *see* Uncertainties facing business
Delta Air Lines, 3, 33, 51, 124, 128, 169, 216
  discovery of revenue management, 34-46
Demographics, 68, 72
Deregulation, 22
  of airline industry, 34, 100, 101, 109
  of telecommunications industry, 152
Downsizing, 1, 5, 11, 216, 257
  described by a victim, 7
  effect on interpretation of data, 24–25
  financial results achieved by, 29
  morale and, 29, 235
  transitory profits from, 8
Drucker, Peter, 187, 244–45
Duke University Medical Center, Diet and Fitness Center, 138–39

Economist, The, 29
EDS (Electronic Data Systems), 245
Educating employees about Revenue Management, 184–85
Employee turnover, 24
Entertainment business, revenue optimization and value cycle of, 89–90
Entropy, 9–12
  external, 10, 11–12
  internal, 10, 11, 62, 235
Ernst & Young, 246

Ethics of Revenue Management, 231–34
External entropy, 10, 11–12

Fain, Richard, 131
Fashion as example of perishable opportunity, 136
Filene's Basement, 136
"First come, first served," 77–78, 79, 231, 234
Fleeting opportunities, capturing, 50–51
Forecasting, 83–85, 175–77
  with computers, 84, 141
  errors in, 84–85
  human factor in, 85
  inability of humans to digest huge amounts of information, 84
  at micromarket level, 141, 142, 146, 148, 157
  optimization based on, *see* Optimization
  reforecasting, continually, 176, 177
  rules of good, 176
Foundation survey, 161
Franz Edelman Award, 213
Free trade, 21
Frontier Airlines, 124
Furniture industry, 77

Game theory, 98
General Electric, 246
General Motors, 18
  National Car Rental and, 191–92, 195, 196, 199, 202, 210, 212
Geraghty, Kevin, 178
Globalization, 21
Grand Metropolitan, 70
Gray, General A. M., 20
Greyhound Bus Lines, 7–9, 21, 103, 167
  entropy affecting, 10–11
Gut feelings, making decisions on, 43, 46, 81, 106
Gwin, Julius, 45

Haan, Phil, 122, 123
Hall, Larry, 173–74
Hamel, Gary, 11
Hammer, Michael, 28
Hanks, Rich, 140–41
Hart, Tim, 203, 208
Hayek, F. A., 50
Health care industry, peak demand periods for, 139
Heinz, 70
Hertz Rent-a-Car, 69, 205–206

Hilton Hotels Corporation, 14, 177, 237
Historical data, information systems making use of, 59–60, 80–85, 168, 170, 175–76
Hospitals, perishable opportunities of, 135
Hotels, 4, 182, 215–16, 220–21
  capital assets used to remedy supply/demand imbalances, 62
  cost-based pricing, 66–67
  no-shows, 146
  perishable opportunities of, 135
  pricing to remedy supply/demand imbalances, 64–65, 140–41
  see also names of individual hotels
Huckestein, Dieter, 14, 16, 237
Human factor, 96–98, 160
  in forecasting, 85
  inability of humans to digest huge amounts of information, 84, 242–43

IBM, 18, 19–20
Implementation plans, 171, 172
  with short-term targets, 172
Individual and bulk purchases, competition between, 149–51
Information, 244, 248, 249
Information explosion, 23–26
Information management, 244
Information technology, 25, 59–60, 80–85
  American Airlines' use of, 109–30
  decision-making machines of the future, 250–54
  designing and building relevant systems, 172–75
  forecasting with, 84, 141
  Marriott Corporation's use of, 141
  National Car Rental's use of, 208–11
  return on investment, 187
  risks of, 228–31
  simulation modeling, 82–83, 169–70, 222, 226, 258
  strengths and weaknesses of computers, 96–98, 160
  viewing the system as a solution, 224–25
INFORMS/CPMS, 213
Institutional fund managers, 18–19
Internal entropy, 10, 11, 62, 235
Internet, 155
Investors, activist, 17–20, 241
ITT, 18

Jay Alix and Associates (JA&A), 199–200
Johnson, Ernest, 196–97, 205–207, 209–10
Just-in-time (JIT) inventory, 27

Kahn, Dr. Alfred, 49
Kelleher, Herb, 159
Knowledge, 243–47, 248, 249
  decision-making based on, 80–85
  going beyond, 247–50
Knowledge management, 246–47
Knowledge workers, 245
Kretz, Peter, 3, 155
Kroc, Ray, 20

Legarreta, Jimmy, 55–57
Livingston, Jack, 198, 199
Lloyd's Aviation Economist, 217
Lobeck, William, 212
Lorenzo, Frank, 123–24, 125
Low-tech example of Revenue Management, 55–57
Lufthansa, 102
Luxury items, 15–16

McDonald's Corporation, 20
McKenna, Bob, 149, 196, 199
McKinnon, Tony, 218–19
McKinsey & Co., 245, 246
Magazine publishers, 147
Management gurus, 27–30, 31, 254–55
Manufacturing, 4
  product wastage, 146–47
  supply/demand imbalances, handling of, 62
Market-based pricing, 66–71, 138–40, 143–46, 154
  ethics of, 232–34
Market-centric focus, 31, 64
Market fragmentation, 14
Marketing renaissance, 237–57
  application of science to marketing, 241–43
  leaders of, 254–57
  marketing-driven business, 238–39, 254–55
  Revenue Management at center of, 241–42
Market research, 15, 239, 240
Market segmentation, *see* Segmented micromarkets, selling to
Marriott, Bill, Jr., 3, 141
Marriott Corporation, 64–65, 140–41
  DFS (Demand Forecasting System), 141

Marshall, Sir Colin, 255
Mass market, 238, 239
MCI, 152
Measuring progress, 186–88, 225–26
Meinke, Carol, barbershop of, 52–55,
    64, 138, 143, 160, 231
Micromarkets:
    analysis of, 40
    forecasting at level of, 141, 142, 146,
    148
    selling to segmented, *see* Segmented
    micromarkets, selling to
Microsoft, 155
"Midnight sales," 76
Milestones, 186
Misguided or misinformed efforts at
    Revenue Management, 218–21
Mistakes in adopting Revenue
    Management techniques, *see*
    Pitfalls in adopting Revenue
    Management techniques
Morale, 29, 235
Mossel, Patricia, 55
Murphy, Tom, 196

National Car Rental System, 3
    case study, 191–213
    champion of Revenue Management
    at, 205–208
    decentralized pricing strategy, 200–
    201
    Emerald Aisle concept, 194–95
    implementation plan, 202–203
    interim system for (Phase .5), 202–
    204, 207–208, 209–10, 212
    leveraged buyout of, 194
    needs evaluation, 198, 199, 200
    objectives for Revenue Management
    at, 201–202
    Phase 1 of project for, 204, 211, 212
    results of Revenue Management for,
    212–13
    snag in developing information
    technology for, 208–11
NBC, 155
NCR, 107–108
Needs evaluation, 161, 164–65, 170–
    71
Nestle, 70
Netcom, 155
Niggley, Dick, 170
Nike, 238
Nonconformist consumers, 13–17
Northwest Airlines, 34
No-shows and overbooking, 105–106,
    146, 147

No-tech example of Revenue
    Management, 52–55

Objectives, setting clear and
    manageable, 163, 186–88
    failure to set objectives, 222–23
Office Max, 15
Opportunity costs, 172–73, 227
    perishable products and, 134–37
Optimal timing, maximizing revenue
    through, 91–92, 137, 148, 157
Optimization, 178–79
Order effects, 24
Organizational structure, practices, and
    processes, 206–207
    evaluating, 165–68
    paying attention to, 224–25
    revenue side of management
    structure, 254–57
Organizational structure, practices, and
    processes, evaluating, 165–68
Overbooking and no-shows, 105–106,
    146, 147

Packard Bell, 143
PanAm, 34, 218–19
PARC, 246
Parides, Michael, 82–83
PC manufacturers, recognition of value
    of product in different market
    segments by, 143–44
Peak demand periods, 137–42
Pension Fund of the International
    Brotherhood of Teamsters, 18
PeopleExpress, 34, 99, 100–108, 114,
    115, 116–26, 215, 217
    American Airlines' Ultimate Super
    Saver fares and, 116–23, 129
    end of, 125–26, 129
    no-shows and overbooking, 105–106
    reservations system, 102–103, 105,
    107–108, 129
    travel agency distribution network
    and, 102, 106–107
Performing arts organizations, 55–57,
    149–50
Perishable products and opportunities,
    134–37
Philips, 239
Pitfalls in adopting Revenue
    Management techniques, 221–28
    failure to measure revenue
    performance, 225–26
    failure to quantify expected benefits,
    221–22

lack of coherent market segmentation plan, 227–28
lack of well-defined plan, 222–23
paralysis by analysis, 224
senior management, lack of oversight of, 223–24
technical staff taking over, 226–27
viewing the system as a solution, 224–25
Post-Capitalist Society (Drucker), 244–45
Prahalad, C. K., 11
Prices and pricing:
  average price for average consumer, 73
  balancing supply/demand imbalances with pricing, 61–65, 137, 140–41, 142
  cost-based, 66–68
  discounting to meet competition, 151–54
  ethics of market-driven pricing, 232–34
  market-based, 66–71, 138–40, 143–46, 154
    ethics of, 232–34
  significance to consumers, 15–16
Price sensitivity analysis, 145
Privatization, 21
Procter & Gamble, 155–56, 238
Production-driven business, 238
Productivity, 102, 247
Product wastage, 146–48
  defined, 146
  examples of, 146–48
  minimizing, 148
Professional services as perishable opportunities, 135
Provincetown-Boston Airlines, 124
Psychographics, 68, 72
Publishing industry, 147

Quaker Company, 70
Quantifying the benefits of Revenue Management, 168–72
  failure to take the time for, 221–22

Radisson Park Terrace, 66–67
Railroads, 4
Ramaekers, Larry, 3, 11, 191, 199–200, 202, 203, 208, 209, 212–13
Reengineering, 1, 27–29, 162
Reengineering the Corporation (Hammer), 28

Reevaluating revenue opportunities, continually, 93–97
Repurchase guarantees for unsold products, 147
Resistance to change, 171, 185, 198, 199, 204–205
Restaurants, 68–69
  cancellation fees, 146
  market segmentation by, 78–79
  no-shows, 146
  peak demand periods of, 137
  perishable opportunities of, 135
  recognizing value of product in different market segments, 144
Retailers, peak demand periods for, 137
Revenue accounting, 220
Revenue audit, 161–62
Revenue Management (RM), 32
  applicability of, to your business, 131–33, 159
  as art and science, 46–47, 162–63
  case studies, *see* Case studies
  as competitive weapon, 215–18
  constraints on successful program, 171–72
  core concepts of, *see* Core concepts of Revenue Management
  as core process, 174–75
  costs of generating new revenue, 179
  defined, 4, 51–52, 131–32
  diagnosing your company's potential for, 159–69
  downside risks of, 228–31
  ethics of, 231–34
  examples of, 52–60
    case studies, *see* Case studies
    high-tech approach, 58–60
    low-tech approach, 55–57
    no-tech approach, 52–55
  external market addressed by, 5
  industries adopting, *see* *individual industries*
  launching the revenue rocket, 159–89
  misguided or misinformed efforts, 218–21
  mistakes, potential, *see* Pitfalls in adopting Revenue Management techniques
  origin of concept, 3
  reducing uncertainties, *see* Uncertainties facing business
  results achieved by, 4, 55, 57, 60, 77, 179, 187, 221
  risks of, 171, 228–31

successful program, steps to, *see*
  Successful RM program, steps to
uncertainties in decision making,
  reducing, *see* Uncertainties facing
  business
Revenue Management attitude, 51–60,
  159–60, 257–59
Revenue Management department, 180
Revenue officer, chief (CRO), 255–57
Revenue targets, setting, 168–72
Right Associates, 29
Risk shifting, 233–34
Risks of Revenue Management, 171,
  228–31
Robinson, James, 18
Roper's Public Pulse, 16
Royal Caribbean Cruise Lines, 131

SABRE reservations system, 103, 106–
  107, 110, 112, 115, 245
Sales-driven business, 238
Sam's Club, 15
Schwarzkopf, General Norman, 163
Sea-Land, 79–80
Seasonal and other peak demands,
  137–42
Segmented micromarkets, selling to,
  71–77
  by American Airlines, 112–14
  lack of coherent market segmentation
    plan, 227–28
  low-tech approaches, 76
  value of products in different
    segments, 142–46, 149–51, 154
  willingness to pay, segmenting
    markets by, 75–76
Shareholders, activist, 17–20, 241
Shipping companies, 62–64, 79–80
Simulation modeling, 82–83, 169–70,
  222, 226, 258
Skills set for Revenue Management
  team, 183, 184
Smith, Adam, 50
Smith, Barry, 119–20
Sony, 238
Southwest Airlines, Inc., 159
Sports team ticket sales, 143, 149–50
Sprint, 152
Stagl, Michael, 60
Stealth competition, 21
Stempel, Robert, 18
Successful RM program, steps to, 163–
  89
  applying optimization, 178–79
  enlisting technology, 172–75
  evaluating success, 186–88

execute, execute, execute, 185–86
  implementing forecasting, 175–77
  market needs, evaluating your, 164–
    65
  organization and processes,
    evaluating your, 165–68
  quantifying the benefits, 168–72
  summary of, 163–64
  teams, creating, 179–85
Supply/demand imbalances:
  capital assets used to balance, 61–62,
    138
  focusing on price when balancing,
    61–65, 137, 140–41, 142
Support from senior management, 179–
  85
  lack of, 223
Swope, Steve, 181, 228
Systems Reengineering Economics, 28

Teams, creating, 179–85
Technical staff, conflicts with, 210–11,
  226–27
Telecommunications industry:
  discounting to meet competition, 152
  perishable opportunities of, 135
Tests to determine a company's
  revenue-generating capabilities,
  160–62
Theaters, peak demand periods of, 137
Theme parks, seasonal demand periods
  of, 138
Total quality control (TQC), 27
Total quality management (TQM), 27,
  29, 162
Training for Revenue Management
  team, 183, 184
Travel agencies and airline ticket sales,
  102, 106–107, 110
Trucking industry, 216
TWA, 34, 128

Uncertainties facing business, 134–57
  competition between individual and
    bulk purchases, 149–51
  discounting to meet competition,
    151–54
  perishable products and
    opportunities, 134–37
  product wastage, 146–48
  rapidly changing circumstances, 154–
    57
  seasonal and other peak demands,
    137–42
  summary of, 134

value of product in different market
    segments, 142–46
Unilever, 238
United Airlines, 34, 124, 126, 128
    reservations system, 103
"Uses of Knowledge in a Society, The,"
    50
Utilities, 4, 22

Valuable customers, saving products for
    most, 77–80, 151
Value:
    consumer demand for, 16
    product's value in different market
        segments, 142–46

Value cycle of a product, exploiting,
    85–92
Virtual nesting, 228–30

Wall Street Journal, The, 4–5, 116,
    150, 216
Warfighting (Gray), 20
Washington Opera, 55–57
Wasik, Vincent, 194–96
Wealth of Nations (Smith), 50
Wisdom, 248–50
Wolf, Stephen M., 257

Xerox, 246

Yield/load factor seesaw, 37, 42, 45